Look What Entrepreneurs, Business Owners, Investors, and Advisors Are Saying About This Gem of a Book

"Philip's approach to financial forecasting has helped us completely turn around our profitability and cash flow and get it moving in a positive direction. I love the way he speaks and writes in a way that is simple and easy-to-understand. The principles in *A Quick Start Guide to Financial Forecasting* have become an integral part of how we plan and manage our financial future every month."

—Andrea Sato, Chief Executive Officer,
Gary's Vacuflo, Inc.

"Cut out the chart **Building a Financially Strong Business** in the bonus chapter. Pin it, tape it, or post it where you can see it daily. Follow every step on there. Then use what Philip teaches in this book to make it happen. It will help turn your business into a secure, financially strong generator of CASH."

—Stan Touchstone, Owner,
Kissimmee Valley Feed and Ranch Supply, Inc.

"*A Quick Start Guide to Financial Forecasting* takes a natural law 'What you focus on you are more likely to achieve' and translates it into a practical tool for improving your financial performance in business. Philip is your expert guide to using this often-overlooked tool, a reliable financial forecast, to create the view through the financial windshield of your business. You are going to love the tips and tools he shares in the book."

—Larry Tyler, Business Advisor,
Author, *Romancing the Loan*

"Thought provoking and detailed. Not only does Philip explain how to prepare a financial forecast, but he also helps you to understand the value and benefits of forecasting."

—Joanna Vu, CPA

"Philip Campbell has a special knack for helping business owners uncover financial insights that others miss. *A Quick Start Guide to*

Financial Forecasting is a brilliant example of his talent for helping entrepreneurs use insightful, forward-looking financial information to develop a bigger and brighter financial future for their company."

—ED LETTE, FOUNDER, PRESIDENT AND CEO,
BUSINESS BANK OF TEXAS

"This book provides an incredibly useful tool for entrepreneurs and finance people alike. It paints a compelling picture of the power of developing a more forward-thinking approach to financial performance. And I love the bonus chapter on how to assess the quality of a company's accounting department. Very enlightening!"

—PATRICK FINN, CPA, PRINCIPAL, FINNANCIAL GROUP, LLC

"Many business owners and managers exhaust themselves and their employees trying to overcome strategic problems with brute force in their day-to-day efforts. They're working hard and moving fast, but they're moving in the wrong direction. As a CPA and consultant to small/medium-sized construction and manufacturing firms, I see this with nearly every new client. They've run themselves ragged trying to figure out what's been happening to their business in recent years. When they finally approach our firm and the first question from me is about their forward operational planning and not about their historical numbers it comes as a shock.

This is nearly always the case; businesses are trying to compensate for their lack of strategic planning and forecasting with short-term Band-Aids and feel-good, immediate solutions that at best prolongs the problem and at worse dooms the business to failure in the long term. That's why the principles and tools in *A Quick Start Guide to Financial Forecasting* are so important to business owners and managers. Whether this is your first exposure to forecasting or you're a seasoned CFO with a talented FP&A staff, reading and applying these principles will seriously sharpen your financial skillset.

By providing clear motivation for why any business over a couple million in revenue needs a forecast, a clear process to create a forecast, and removal of common barriers to forecasting,

Mr. Campbell has penned a recipe for forecasting success and proven this recipe with examples throughout the book. Use what you learn from this book to speak with confidence to your lenders and investors when approaching expectations for coming months. Make better strategic decisions like expanding into new sales territories or shutting down an operation. Use a forecast as a bellwether to know if bad times are approaching.

I'm recommending *A Quick Start Guide to Financial Forecasting* to my clients and I highly recommend you read it too."

—JAMES H. JOHNSON, CPA, CITP, CGMA, MBA,
TRAINER, WRIGHT, & PATERNO CPAs

"The same way a pilot creates a flight plan and checks the weather forecast along their route, *A Quick Start Guide to Financial Forecasting* provides the view of where you want to take your business and helps you plan the route that will get you there safely and on time."

—ALI A. MOHAMMED,
MANAGING DIRECTOR, RAMCO INTERNATIONAL (U) LTD

"Philip Campbell has a unique talent for taking complex financial subjects and simplifying them so that every business can benefit. His knowledge and background are apparent in his depth of understanding of such difficult financial subjects as cash flow and forecasting. I have added *A Quick Start Guide to Financial Forecasting* to my list of required reading for entrepreneurs and business owners—a list which already includes Philip's first book *Never Run Out of Cash*."

—MARK A. ADAM B.A., B.Sc., M.B.A.,
LECTURER (SESSIONAL) IN FINANCE,
SCHOOL OF BUSINESS AND ECONOMICS,
THOMPSON RIVERS UNIVERSITY

"I enjoyed the focus on simplicity and the value of treating the forecasting process as a top-down exercise. The book provides specific tips and tools for those new to forecasting as well as the seasoned forecaster."

—JENNIE ENHOLM, CPA, CGMA

"I enjoyed and was challenged by the 'think top-down, not bottom-up' approach Philip Campbell teaches in this book. It will change the way you think as a business owner and help you drive different behavior throughout your company. *A Quick Start Guide to Financial Forecasting* is easy-to-read and provides engaging stories and examples you will find very relatable…and actionable.

I believe a business owner that is making some money, but not getting where he/she really wants to be, will benefit the most from this book. Sometimes business owners find themselves depressed for not having done 'all the right things'. This book will inspire you to buckle down, take steps to create a reliable, top down overview and forecast, then hone in on where your business is truly going. THEN you can align it to where YOU want it to go!

I also believe that business owners that might not be making money, those that may have overpaid for their business or are overleveraged, will discover that Philip's approach to financial forecasting will play a large role in their recovery."

—JOHN ALBERS, PRESIDENT/CEO, THE ALBERS GROUP, LLC

A Quick Start Guide to Financial Forecasting

A Quick Start Guide to Financial Forecasting

---

*Discover the secret to
driving growth, profitability,
and cash flow higher*

Philip Campbell

Grow and Succeed Publishing

This book is dedicated to John Jones, Steve Harter, Cary Vollintine, Finn Thoresen, and Chris Atayan. Over the course of my career, these CEOs helped me become a shareholder in their companies and share in the value they were creating. I absolutely love being a shareholder in great businesses. It creates a huge sense of pride that I thoroughly enjoy and value. Thank you very much for the trust you have shown in me and allowing me to be a shareholder in your company.

Table of Contents

Foreword

By Steve Player

If you lead an organization or work to support that leader, you are often faced with deciding what should be done next. That decision is easier to make if you knew what was going to happen in the future. Yet understanding the future is clouded by an increasingly complex world that seems to be moving faster and faster with an ever-expanding array of options. If this task leaves your head spinning, you have come to the right place. This book will get you started on understanding how financial forecasting can help you and your organization improve decision making.

Many finance organizations struggle in helping to support decision makers. They spend the vast majority of their time diligently working to accurately close the books. Accurate financial statements are needed but in most cases they are after-the-fact confirmations of decisions already made. Although this work is important it can crowd out more useful approaches.

Many finance teams seek to speed up the closing of their books. Even if highly successful, operational managers are left with trying to drive forward while looking at the rearview mirror. Progressive finance teams are turning this around and using the entire front windshield to help guide the organization. This book will help you do a better job of looking forward.

How can organizations of any size–small, medium, or large–do a better job of being prepared for whatever might come their way? Many have successfully answered this question by shifting their focus to forward-looking forecasting. This book will show you how you and your organization can get started.

What I like about Philip's book is the very practical way it helps organizations get started in forecasting. Many organizations are overwhelmed by the vast array of potential drivers they could use. Some who have tried to use rolling forecasts get lost trying to create the perfect predictive logic diagram. This book takes a simpler approach. It reduces complexity by simply asking what two numbers can you multiply together to forecast the direction of your business. By starting with the simple equation of price multiplied by quantity, virtually any business can get started with forecasting quickly.

For those who think this is too simplistic, I remember what Zig Ziglar once told me. He said, "Anything worth doing is worth doing poorly–until you can learn how to do it well." The basic approach presented in this book will help your organization get started regardless of size. My experience is that it is much easier to refine and improve a model than to discuss it in abstract.

As you and your team work with live financial models, it will be much easier to refine those models adding additional insights and knowledge. Working with real data to continuously improve your model provides faster time to benefits and helps you test different potential factors. It may be the quickest way to fully discover the algorithms of your business.

The hands-on approach used in this book will quickly show you the math behind forecasting calculations. There is a specific chapter showing how numbers flow across all the projected statements of income and expense, assets and liabilities, and cash flows. You can work these in the book or download the supporting schedules from the book's website.

This book will show how to leverage your historical financial statements to validate whether your forecasts are realistic based on your history. It provides a way to test potential alternative strategies.

Finance organizations are learning that they must stop doing dumb stuff like taking three to six months to complete an annual budget, wasting time on monthly budget variations when the budget was based on assumptions that have long since turned stale, and driving everything off a financial cycle instead of the natural business cycle. Today's world is moving toward twenty-first-century technology, which allows continuous monitoring of operations, real-time reconciliation of cash accounts at any point they are needed, and the need for finance teams to stand on the bridge of the ship next to the leaders of the business. That way they help decide what to do in the future instead of being stuck on the back of the ship counting what has happened in the past.

To be ready for this world we need forward-looking, driver-based rolling forecasts telling us what will most likely happen. But because the future is not certain a great finance organization will also have several scenario plans of what could happen instead—with both upside and downside contingencies. For the upside opportunities, we will have plans to seize those opportunities before our competitors. For the downside risks, we will have plans to protect our organization and properly position it for any fallout. In all cases, we will also be looking at leading indicators that tell us which reality is becoming more likely and when we need to swing into action.

This book will not show you how to perfectly predict the future. I have not seen a book that can do that. But this book will get you started on a journey to better understand what has happened and what could happen. And if you use this book to help your organization develop plans to deal with both the upside and the downside, then you will be well on your way to the goal, which is to Live Future Ready!

I look forward to seeing you on the journey.

Best Regards,

STEVE PLAYER
MARCH 17, 2017
DALLAS, TEXAS
AUTHOR, *Future Ready: How to Master Business Forecasting*
DIRECTOR, BEYOND BUDGETING ROUND TABLE NORTH AMERICA
MANAGING DIRECTOR, LIVE FUTURE READY

"A business, like an automobile, has to be driven in order to get results."

B. C. Forbes

About the Author

 Philip Campbell is the Senior Vice President of Planning at AMCON Distributing Company, a public company on the New York Stock Exchange. AMCON is a leading wholesale distributor of consumer products and also operates sixteen health and natural product retail stores in the Midwest and Florida. Philip is the author of the book ***Never Run Out of Cash: The 10 Cash Flow Rules You Can't Afford to Ignore.*** The book is an easy-to-understand, step-by-step guide for business owners and managers who want to better understand and manage their cash flow.

Philip is also the author of the online course ***Understanding Your Cash Flow–In Less Than 10 Minutes.*** The course teaches a simplified approach to understanding and managing cash flow each month.

Philip's career began in public accounting. He was a staff accountant in a local CPA firm in Beaumont, Texas, and then an audit manager in an international accounting firm in Houston, Texas.

Since 1990, he has served as a financial officer in a number of growing companies with revenues ranging from $5 million to over $1 billion. He has been involved in the acquisition or sale of 33 companies and an IPO on the New York Stock Exchange.

What really sets Philip apart from the average financial person you meet is his passion and excitement about helping entrepreneurs and CEOs win financially in business. Philip believes strongly that growing a successful business makes it critical that management knows exactly what's going on with their cash flow. In fact, early on in his career, he focused and "preached" so much about the importance of cash flow that people now call him **CASH**.

He lives in Round Rock, Texas.

Website FinancialRhythm.com
Philip Campbell's Blog http://campbellphilip.typepad.com/
Phone 512 944 3520
Email pcampbell@financialrhythm.com
Twitter @cashflowrules

Introduction

"If you don't know where you are going, any road will get you there."
—LEWIS CARROLL, *ALICE IN WONDERLAND*

The purpose of this book is to give you a straightforward, easy-to-implement guide to using one of the most powerful financial tools in business: **a reliable financial forecast**.

Creating the forward-looking view of financial performance is a surprisingly effective way to transform the financial future of your company. It will:

- Help you drive growth, profitability, and cash flow higher.
- Create confidence and clarity about where your business is going financially.
- Provide the roadmap for turning your vision and strategy for your business into a crystal clear view of what success should look like financially.
- Enhance confidence and credibility with lenders and investors so they provide the capital and support you need to grow your business.
- Help you make more courageous, confident, and profitable financial decisions.

In short, a reliable financial forecast will help you win in business.

Put yourself in the driver's seat by tapping into the unique and exciting benefits that financial forecasting can unlock for you.

Too many entrepreneurs today are feeling more like passengers than drivers in their business. They're staring at their rearview mirror as they bounce along in the passenger seat. Oftentimes their company is careening along on the highway of business as they wonder and worry about where their business might end up financially.

But, as B. C. Forbes, the founder of *Forbes Magazine*, said:

> *"A business, like an automobile, has to be driven*
> *in order to get results."*

Just like an automobile, your business can be driven in a way that is reckless and scary…or wise and cautious. It can be driven fast or it can be driven slow. But the business "has to be driven in order to get results." The business is going *somewhere*. The million dollar question is *where is your business going?* And will you arrive at your intended destination safely and on time?

A reliable financial forecast will help you create the visibility and clarity you need to drive your company toward a bigger and brighter financial future. It will reward you and your management team in exciting and surprising ways. And it will pay huge dividends for everyone interested in, or invested in, the financial success of your company.

Looking Through Your Financial Windshield

This book is not a math-based deep dive into the intricacies of financial modeling. It's about a common-sense approach for entrepreneurs and CEOs who want to use forward-looking financial information to make better business decisions. Whether you want to do the actual forecasting work yourself or not, I'll show you the benefits and a systematic approach to seeing more clearly through the financial windshield of your business.

It's really easy to run a business day-to-day and end up spending most of your time looking through the rearview mirror (by exclusively focusing on historical financial statements). As a result, questions like these go unanswered:

- What does the future of my company look like financially?
- What does the view through the company's *financial windshield* look like?
- How much cash can we distribute to owners this year?
- How much cash will we generate in the coming months or years to pay down debt?
- How long will it take to pay off our debt?
- What do our profitability and cash flow look like by month over the next six to eighteen months?
- If we achieve our growth plans over the next few years, how much more valuable will the company be than it is today?

As you begin your financial forecasting journey, some new questions will pop up like:

- Do you understand your business model well enough to create a forecast or projection of what is likely to happen in the coming months?

- Can you identify the areas of uncertainty that your management team must deal with in order to hit your financial targets?
- Do you have a plan for mitigating the risks that could derail your growth plans?
- How are you going to exploit existing opportunities to grow and improve your profitability and cash flow?

Once you put a reliable financial forecast in place, the answers to these questions will jump off the page at you. Decision making will become more focused. Accountability will skyrocket. Financial surprises will diminish. It will make your job as CEO or business owner a lot easier…and a lot more effective and rewarding.

WINNING IN BUSINESS IS FUN…AND REWARDING

I have had the privilege of working with some amazing entrepreneurs and CEOs over the last thirty years. I refer to them as serious-minded entrepreneurs and CEOs. I've seen firsthand the enormous passion and commitment they have for their company.

I define a serious-minded entrepreneur or CEO as a person running a company who pays close attention to the two "factories" that exist in every business: the **customer factory** and the **money factory**. The customer factory is the part of the business dedicated to creating happy *customers*. A happy customer is a customer that loves your products and services, comes back often, and refers their friends and associates to you. The money factory is the part of your business dedicated to creating happy *owners*. A happy owner is an owner who receives healthy (and predictable) cash distributions from the business. A serious-minded entrepreneur is focused on both their customer factory *and* their money factory. Either by taking the lead themselves in each area or by having a strong management team and advisors dedicated to making sure both sides of the business are operating together as a well-oiled machine.

I bet you are just like them.

- Your financial future, and the financial future of your family, is riding on the success of your business.
- Winning in business is one of your highest priorities right now.
- You love your company and the unique challenges and opportunities it presents.
- You own a big chunk of the company and you have a passion for making it bigger and better every year.
- Deep down you know that your business must grow financially in order to turn your vision of success into reality.
- You've decided to turn the accounting and financial side of your business into a strategic asset that can help you grow and make more money.

I Love Business

I discovered early in my career that working with entrepreneurs and CEOs like you was part of my calling in business. I witnessed your love of business and your willingness to take risks to achieve your vision for your company. You have a unique ability to motivate people, you know how to get and keep customers, and you work relentlessly and tirelessly to make your company better and better every month.

I remember saying to myself many years ago, "I love business and there are smart entrepreneurs out there growing exciting companies. I understand how they think and I know the downsides they will experience if they allow the financial side of the business to underperform. I can mix my love of business with my unique approach to the accounting and financial side of the business to form a combination with CEOs that is both fun and rewarding for everyone involved. That's my calling!"

I'm a 55-year-old CPA and financial officer who absolutely loves business and the challenge of making money. I've spent the last thirty years helping entrepreneurs and CEOs like you build, improve, buy, and sell great businesses. I've built a rewarding career by teaming up with smart CEOs and helping them grow and achieve their financial goals. It puts a big smile on my face just thinking (and writing) about it.

As a young CPA, I learned quickly that the key to adding value was helping business owners and executives understand what's going on *below the surface* of their financial statements. Later, as a CFO, I discovered the power of creating the forward-looking view of financial performance for CEOs. I learned that when you put insightful and action-oriented financial information in front of a smart CEO amazing things begin to happen in their business.

I've seen the surprise and delight on their face when they get visibility into what's about to happen financially rather than just seeing information about the past. It opens their eyes to the power of clarity and insight about the future. They begin to view financial information in a whole new light. They even begin paying closer attention to their financial statements. They discover the importance of identifying and focusing on the key drivers of financial performance. And not long after that, results begin to improve. Profitability and cash flow accelerate. The company begins to grow. And that puts a big smile on *everyone's* face.

THE TWO QUESTIONS YOU MUST ANSWER EVERY MONTH

You need to ask, and answer, two simple questions about the *financial side* of your business at the end of every month:

1. What happened (last month)?
2. What's about to happen (in the coming months)?

You need to have the information available to you to answer those two questions quickly…every month.

A well-designed monthly reporting package (with easy-to-understand historical financial statements and insight about results vs. plan) will help you answer the first question.

A reliable financial forecast will help you answer the second question. It will tell you instantly if your company is on track to achieve your financial goals or if you need to intervene in a specific area of the business.

When I am operating in a CFO or consultant role, it's my job to deliver financial information that answers those two questions in a simple, easy-to-understand fashion. In less than two minutes, you want to know how your business performed against your plan and what's likely to happen in the coming months. That's the objective of a well-designed monthly reporting package together with a reliable financial forecast.

IT'S ALL ABOUT DECISION MAKING, NOT PRECISION

Picture this in your mind. You are in Honolulu, Hawaii (one of my favorite places to spend time–you should put it on your travel list if you have not been there, or if you have not been there recently). Here's the weather you are enjoying on a beautiful Sunday afternoon as you admire the awesome view of Diamond Head on Waikiki Beach (this was in December).

HAWAII WEATHER FORECAST

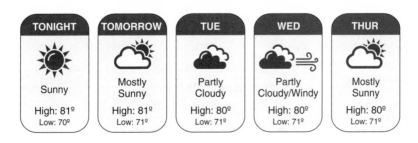

TONIGHT	TOMORROW	TUE	WED	THUR
Sunny	Mostly Sunny	Partly Cloudy	Partly Cloudy/Windy	Mostly Sunny
High: 81º	High: 81º	High: 80º	High: 80º	High: 80º
Low: 70º	Low: 71º	Low: 71º	Low: 71º	Low: 71º

But you are leaving for Flagstaff, Arizona on Monday. (Why you would want to leave Hawaii in December is a whole different issue–the Humpback whales are just arriving–and whale watching in Hawaii, especially when you do some island hopping to Maui, is super-fun).

You need to make some decisions about what to pack. So, you pull up the weather forecast for Flagstaff and it says:

FLAGSTAFF WEATHER FORECAST

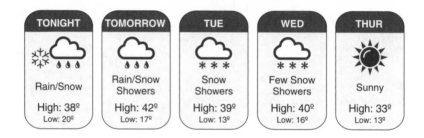

(Not everyone realizes Flagstaff is 7,000 feet above sea level even though it is in Arizona. Average annual snowfall there is about 100 inches.)

Is a weather forecast always going to be *exactly* right? Nope.

Is it *likely* to be cold and wet where you are going? Yep.

Is there any question what kind of clothes you should pack for your trip? Nope.

The question *isn't* whether the forecasted temperature is exactly right or if the exact day of the snow is right. The question is "What kind of clothes should I pack?" The forecast shows that it will likely snow and be very cold and wet on the front end of your trip. The forecast gives you enough information to make a smart decision about what to pack for your trip. That's where the forecast brings value. It helps you make better decisions. The value of the forecast is in painting a picture of what you are likely to experience when you arrive in Flagstaff so you can make wise decisions *before* you leave Hawaii.

THE PANORAMIC VIEW

Let's say you decide to visit the Grand Canyon during your visit to Flagstaff. You are looking out over the South Rim and you want to take a picture to capture the beauty you are surrounded by and share it with your friends and family. But it's hard to capture the complete beauty in front of you in a single photograph. The beautiful view spans from your far left to your far right. So, you use the special panoramic feature of your smartphone (or camera) to capture more of the beautiful view.

Merriam-Webster defines panorama as "a picture exhibited a part at a time by being unrolled before the spectator; an unobstructed or complete view of an area in every direction; a comprehensive presentation of a subject." In photography, capturing the panoramic view is a way to "stitch together" multiple images to create a single, wide photograph. In essence, you are able to capture a more complete view of the beauty in front of you.

Traditional financial statements are that single, non-panoramic, picture of financial performance in the past. The "panoramic view" of financial performance includes a reliable financial forecast so you have the more complete view of what's about to happen financially. A reliable financial forecast helps you "stitch together" the wider, more panoramic view of your financial performance. Why settle for that single snapshot of the past when you have a tool available to you to capture a complete view of your financial past, present, *and* future?

> "We are all forecasters. When we think about changing jobs, getting married, buying a home, making an investment, launching a product, or retiring, we decide based on how we expect the future will unfold. These expectations are forecasts."
>
> —Philip E. Tetlock and Dan Gardner, *SuperForecasting*

A Fun Little Experiment

Take a minute to try this fun little experiment. Stand up, cover your eyes with both hands, and then try to walk slowly to the opposite side of the room without bumping into something. Even in a room you are familiar with, it is very uncomfortable to walk across the room with both hands covering your eyes without running into something.

Now try it again…but this time separate your fingers just a tiny bit so you can see a little bit of light between your fingers. That little bit of visibility between your fingers is enough to help you walk safely across the room without bumping into something. That's what a reliable financial forecast is all about. It's not about providing *complete* visibility or certainty. It's about providing a little *glimpse* of what lies ahead so you increase the likelihood of reaching your destination safely.

It's like driving your car at night. You can only see as far as your headlights…but that's all you need. You can make your whole trip that way. It doesn't matter if your drive is five miles or five hundred miles. Shining a light on the road immediately ahead of you is all you need in order to get where you are going safely.

Your Role in the Business

If you have a CFO on your team, great. This book provides them the step-by-step process they can implement for you. It also shows a CFO how to use financial forecasting to increase their personal credibility and influence inside your company so they can play a more strategic and vital role in the future of your company.

If you don't have a dedicated CFO on your team, that doesn't mean your company doesn't have a CFO. You have one all right. It's YOU. (The million-dollar question is whether you're a CFO Rock Star or not.) You will need to learn how to implement the forecasting process I have set out for you. Or you can get some help from someone inside, or outside, your company to do it.

Either way, one of the benefits you will receive by reading this book is it provides you the roadmap for how a seasoned CFO can create true and lasting value for your company. This roadmap will come in very handy as your company grows and you begin looking for a dedicated CFO to add to your leadership team in the future.

CPAs, accountants, bookkeepers, and consultants who serve businesses will benefit from financial forecasting as well. The business owners and entrepreneurs you serve are starving for more insightful and action-oriented financial information. Helping clients see what's about to happen financially is a powerful way for you to add value. It helps you move past just providing the traditional financial statements or a tax return for your clients and begin to make a true and lasting impact on your client's business and its financial future.

WALKING THROUGH THE FORECASTING PROCESS

Here's how we'll walk through the financial forecasting process in this book:

1. Highlight the benefits of financial forecasting. This section speaks to the WHYs and purpose of forecasting. Specifically, why forecasting is the single most powerful tool to include in your financial toolkit if you are serious about creating financial success.
2. Show you the step-by-step process for planning, creating, and presenting your financial forecast. We'll talk about the common mistakes that people make in forecasting so you can avoid the pitfalls. I'll provide you the recipe to follow as you create your first forecast.
3. Provide you with next steps and tips on how to overcome the obstacles and roadblocks that can get in your way as you get your financial forecasting process up and running.

I have also included two bonus chapters for you.

The first bonus chapter is a 3-part plan for breathing financial life back into your business. It will give you a sensible plan, a roadmap, you can follow that will guide you on your path to building a strong, wealth generating business. This roadmap will guide you along the full financial life cycle of your business.

The second bonus chapter will help you evaluate your accounting and finance function, what some consider a necessary evil, and turn it into an asset the financial community respects and admires and that forms the foundation for helping you grow and succeed financially. Too many entrepreneurs have a weak accounting and financial function in their business. It handcuffs their ability to grow and attract capital and talent. It hurts their credibility with bankers, lenders, investors, partners, and all those in the financial community you need to grow your business successfully. I'll show you how to turn the accounting and financial function within your business into an important strategic asset. An asset that will help you win in business. An asset that will help you create confidence and credibility with all the people interested in, and invested in, the financial success of your company.

Free Downloads and Examples

I have included in the free resources section of the website that supports this book (www.ILoveForecasting.com) several rapid-learning videos so you can watch an example of the forecasting process in action. I pull up my forecasting software tool of choice while you watch the step-by-step process with me explaining a very specific aspect of the forecasting process for you. You can both read and watch how the process works so you know exactly how to get started with your own forecast.

The short, rapid-learning videos are an important part of how I want to add value for you with this book. It will help crystalize the principles in a way that you will really enjoy. I sincerely want you to get value in an amount far, far greater than the time and money you have invested with me. I hope it will make the information easy to understand and easy to implement.

"Life is very much like a buffet line. Life is self-serve. Nobody brings it to you. You cannot sit at the table and bang your knife and fork for service. You have to get up, accept responsibility, and serve yourself.

If you want to get to the front of the buffet line of life, two steps are necessary. First, get in line! Make a decision to be excellent at what you do and then get in line. From that moment on, do something every day to improve. Second, stay in line. Don't make an occasional attempt at personal improvement and then go back and watch television. Get in line and stay in line.

Keep putting one foot in front of the other. Learn and practice new things every single day. Keep moving forward. Never lose your momentum."

—Brian Tracy, *Focal Point*

In the videos (and throughout the book), I will focus on modeling a full set of financial statements. We are not just forecasting profit. We are going to create a forecast that includes an income statement, balance sheet, and statement of cash flows. We want a full set of financial statements so we have a view of what we expect financial results, financial position, and cash flows to look like for the near future. That way we are hooking the overall vision and strategy you have for your company up to the likely financial implications of achieving that strategy.

SMALL HINGES SWING BIG DOORS

Financial forecasting is a powerful business tool all by itself. But what excites me even more is the way a reliable financial forecast opens the door to even bigger benefits in your business. It starts by providing you a clear view of where you are going financially. It shines a light on the dangers and opportunities that lie ahead on your journey to grow and succeed in business.

Then even larger doors begin to swing open.

As you make forecasting a part of your monthly financial rhythm, you begin to develop a deeper understanding of your business model and the key drivers of financial results. It creates clarity for you and your management team about what financial success should look like. It highlights the specific drivers of profitability and cash flow that are ripe for improvement. Your team begins to better understand the financial statements and they start using them as a decision-making tool. It becomes so much easier to respond to the curve balls that business will throw at you from time to time.

Your confidence goes up. Your lenders' and investors' confidence in you goes up. The business becomes easier to manage. You spend less time fighting fires. You reduce risk. You free up more of your time to focus on the parts of your business you enjoy and the areas where you can have the biggest impact.

And it all starts with a reliable financial forecast.

PART ONE

It's All About Driving Growth, Profitability, and Cash Flow Higher

"Money isn't everything. But it ranks right up there with oxygen."

Zig Ziglar

Chapter 1

Thinking Strategically About Financial Success

"The goal of a company is solely in the hands of its owners. So the question 'What is the goal of the enterprise?' is exactly equivalent to the question 'Why did the shareholders invest their money in the enterprise?' In order to achieve what?"

—Eliyahu M. Goldratt, *The Haystack Syndrome: Sifting Information Out of the Data Ocean*

Before we dive too deep into the details of the forecasting process, let's take a quick look at where you stand right now and why financial forecasting is on your radar screen.

I'm willing to bet there's a reason this book has shown up in your life at this moment. There's a reason you are getting serious about creating the view through the financial windshield of your business.

1. **You're focused on driving your profitability, cash flow, and net worth higher.** Your basic personality motivates you to push forward and make things happen in your company. And one of the most basic concepts in improving financial results is that you need to know the score. You need visibility into the key

17

drivers of performance. You need a plan. And you need to monitor your pace and progress against that plan. A reliable financial forecast, together with fast, accurate, and insightful financial information, is a powerful tool for helping you increase profits, improve cash flow, and grow the value of your business (and your personal net worth).

2. **You want to grow your company.** You know that to grow your company you need to build a solid financial foundation to support your growth. Growing a business without a strong financial foundation is what kills many entrepreneurs because they think "Let's go out and grow this thing. Everything will work out if we double revenues." But growing a company has far-reaching implications on your financial position and cash flow. A reliable financial forecast helps you plan for the financial implications of growth so you don't grow yourself right into a cash crisis. (You would be surprised how often this happens to entrepreneurs.)

3. **You're considering raising capital or selling your company in the near future.** Raising capital or thinking about selling your company in the future is a great motivator. They both force you to think about the forward-looking view of financial performance. After you talk to bankers or others in the financial community you quickly realize that anyone interested in lending you money or investing in your business wants to see "the numbers." They want to see what your company looks like on paper. And they want an insightful view into what your financial performance will look like *in the near future*. They want a simple, easy-to-understand view into your future profitability and cash flow.

4. **Your financial results are slowing.** Sometimes poor financial results are the wake-up call that gets you focused on improving your financial performance. Few things create fear, dread, and panic like declining financial results (or a full-blown cash shortage). You need information on the key drivers of performance.

You need fast, accurate, and insightful financial information so you can get everyone in the company focused on fixing the problem. You need a reliable financial forecast to help you define the path forward and provide feedback every month about your progress.

5. **Your accounting department is dragging you down.** One of the attributes of a weak accounting department is the financial statements they provide are both slow and sloppy. As a result, you have been making important decisions based on incomplete financial information. And you are starting to feel the negative effects. Lenders and investors don't trust your financials. They are pushing you to fix the problem. Your credibility is starting to take a hit because they know you are flying blind (financially speaking). There is too much riding on the success of your growth plans to allow your accounting function to perform at levels below what you demand from every other part of your company. A reliable financial forecast is a fantastic tool to help you, and your accounting team to turn your numbers into insight and action.

Pause for just a minute and think about which of these reasons best describes what you want to accomplish with financial forecasting. It will help you get clear about where you are and what you want to accomplish.

Whichever motivation or situation best describes where you are right now, I applaud you for getting started. You are going to be glad you took the leap into forecasting.

THINKING STRATEGICALLY

There are two components to thinking strategically about financial success in business.

1. Thinking strategically about how you *personally* define financial success

2. Thinking strategically about the larger goal of financial forecasting as a tool for helping you grow your company

Let's talk more about each component.

A Personal Example

Let me share an example of what I mean by thinking strategically and how it can influence the way you make decisions day-to-day.

Very early in my career as a CPA, then later as a CFO and financial executive, I developed a philosophy about work. With the benefit of more than thirty years of hindsight, here is how I describe my philosophy:

Make sure I'm worth more than I'm paid.

Making sure you are worth more than you are paid is a contrarian view of work. The more "normal view" is to make sure that you are paid what you *are* worth. The "normal view" says that if your role or value to an organization is $150,000, then you should be paid $150,000.

But I realized early on that I could make more money, and create a more enjoyable career, by going at it differently than most people. I decided to put my attention on growing my value as fast as I could. I wanted to increase my ability to make a difference in the company. I had to take on bigger roles. I had to find ways to help the company make more money. I had to make a real difference for the CEO and the leadership team. *Then* I would work on making my compensation go up.

So I "tied a string" to my compensation. As my value, or contribution, went up the money would follow because they were "tied" together. But I always left some slack in the string. As I added more value and made myself worth more, I did not try to increase my compensation immediately. Usually the money followed my increase in value in fairly short order. Other times I had to "yank on the string" to get my compensation to where it needed to be. Having some slack between the two was a very important part of my strategy.

> "The whole trick to money is having some. There is really nothing else to it. That might sound a bit glib, but only to a person who doesn't have any money. If you have money, you will know that how you got it was by having it."
>
> —Stuart Wilde, *The Trick to Money Is Having Some*

I also identified that I would focus on making money as a CFO in three areas:

1. A healthy salary
2. A heavy emphasis on incentive, performance-based compensation
3. An equity interest in the company where I worked

This was another way I could differentiate myself from most accountants (and most employees in general). I wanted a compensation model that was focused on reaping the rewards of creating value at a high level. It helped me "put my money where my mouth was" with the CEO and owners of the business.

The Value vs. Compensation quadrant in Figure 1-1 is a great way to show you what I mean. (I also use this quadrant with entrepreneurs to help them evaluate their team/employees as well as to facilitate a discussion about how their company adds value for customers.)

The quadrant has four sections. The top right section is **The Sweet Spot**. These people are adding value at a high level and are

Figure 1-1
VALUE VS. COMPENSATION

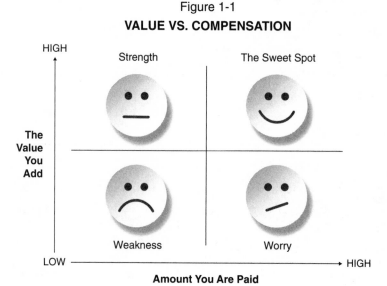

paid well. These are your superstars. This is where I wanted to end up in my career.

The top left section is the **Strength** section. These people are adding value at a high level but are not paid well. It's a position of strength because they have proven they can add value at a high level for the organization. Now they can focus a portion of their energy on turning that ability into higher pay. This is where I put most of my focus early in my career as a young CPA and CFO.

The bottom left section is the **Weakness** section. These people are not adding much value and are not paid very well. This is actually where many people operate because they think in terms of "OK boss, give me a pay increase *then* I will take on the new role/position you want to put me in." It is easy for people to get trapped in this section because they feel taken advantage of because of their low pay. It's a "What comes first, the chicken or the egg" dilemma.

The bottom right section is the **Worry** section. These people add little value but are paid well. It is an uncomfortable place because they know they are getting over on the boss. They are constantly looking over their shoulder. They know the boss is going to come to his or her senses…they just don't know when.

My goal day-to-day was to do my work well. But year-to-year, I had a larger career strategy to guide me on my path toward financial success. It's the same with financial forecasting in that forecasting is a tool that helps you get your work done day to day. But you also have to keep your larger strategic purpose clearly in mind so you are mindful of the larger financial prize you are after in business.

How Do You Define Financial Success?

The first component of thinking strategically, thinking big picture, about financial success is to consider how you *personally* define financial success.

Here are two questions that can help you clarify and define the larger view of what you are trying to achieve financially. Stop for just a minute and jot down your gut-level response to these two questions:

1. Why did you invest money in your company?

_____

_____

_____

2. In order to achieve what financially?

_____

_____

_____

I love these questions because they encourage you to think seriously about what you really want from your business from a financial perspective.

Creating a Strong Net Worth

To me, financial success ultimately comes down to having money. And to *have* money you need to *make* money (which starts with ensuring your business generates strong profitability and cash flow). Then you need to hang on to a portion of that money and invest it wisely so your money continues to grow (growth in the value of your business as well as your other investments).

The path to "having money" is to create a strong net worth. Both personally *and* in your business.

Here is a question that can help you hone in on how big your financial goals are. Do you want to create a net worth of:

- $1,000,000
- $5,000,000
- $10,000,000
- ...or more?

Your net worth goal is not something that you have to think about every day. It's more of an aspirational goal to think through, write down, and reflect on from time to time as you evaluate your progress in building your business. It's one component of thinking strategically (big picture) about what financial success means to you.

The Components of Financial Success

Financially speaking, your challenge in business is to generate above average profitability and cash flow while making your business worth more and more money every year. Figure 1-2 shows how each of these components of financial success fit together.

Figure 1-2
COMPONENTS OF FINANCIAL SUCCESS

Profitability	Cash Flow	Net Worth
✓ Getting and keeping customers	✓ Profitability	✓ Cash flow
✓ Strong margins	✓ Speed of converting assets to cash	✓ Allocating capital wisely
✓ Growth	✓ Capex	✓ Managing risk
✓ Controlling costs	✓ Debt	✓ Driving valuation

Profitability. The ultimate test of your business model is whether you can consistently and predictably get and keep customers. Having strong margins is about selling at a price that provides value for customers and a healthy gross profit for you. Growth is about scaling the business up and touching even more customers. Controlling costs is about keeping expenses in check so you bring a solid percentage of revenues to the bottom line.

Cash flow. Profitability is an important driver of cash flow. But the speed with which you convert assets into cash is also very important. Assets like accounts receivable and inventory have a big impact on cash flow, especially as you grow your business. Capital expenditures (capex) are the purchases you make in the longer term assets necessary to sustain your existing business as well as to invest in future growth. Your debt levels and debt service obligations play a large role in your sources and uses of cash from month-to-month.

Net worth. Allocating your excess cash flow is about deciding how much to retain and re-invest in your business and how much to distribute to owners. That's the beauty of a business that generates excess cash. You have the money to continue to invest and build the company. Or you can distribute some or all of the excess cash flow so the owners can invest in assets outside the business. Both are designed to help you increase your net worth over time.

Your financial success in business will be determined by how well you drive *profitability*...which drives *cash flow*...which drives *net worth*.

Driving profitability, cash flow, and net worth higher over time will ultimately determine whether you *have money* or not. Financial forecasting will help you think seriously and strategically about what needs to happen in each of these areas for your company, and you personally, to become a financial success.

The Strategic Role of Financial Forecasting

Another component of thinking strategically about financial success is to think about the larger goal of financial forecasting as a tool for helping you build your company. A reliable financial forecast will help you:

1. Define where your business is going financially (and where you want it to go).
2. Shine a light on the dangers and opportunities that lie ahead of you on your journey.
3. Create a roadmap to get you there safely and on time.
4. Monitor your pace and progress on your journey to success.

When you know where you are going and you have a plan to get you there safely and on time, you will feel a sense of courage, confidence, and peace of mind. This is why financial forecasting is such a powerful tool in business. In essence, it forces you to think strategically about your business and where you want your business to go. It encourages you to paint a picture of what business and financial success looks like in a way that is revealing and enlightening.

You will be pleasantly surprised by the confidence and courage you feel once you have a reliable financial forecast at work in your business.

Chapter 2

The Benefits of a Reliable Financial Forecast

*"It only takes action on a few insights to improve greatly
the quality of your life."*

—RICHARD KOCH, *THE 80/20 PRINCIPLE*

I've found that starting something new is easier when you have a good view of the benefits that you'll enjoy from making the effort to get started. Getting a clear picture in your mind of the benefits you will enjoy is helpful in motivating you during the hard work phase of forecasting. In addition, knowing the benefits you will enjoy also helps you answer questions like:

- Can forecasting help me increase profits and cash flow quickly?
- Can forecasting help give me the courage and confidence to make better business decisions?
- How will I benefit from making forecasting a part of how I manage my company every month?
- What kinds of business questions will a forecast help me answer?
- What role does forecasting play in my plans to take my company to the next level?

Here are some of the more powerful benefits of a reliable financial forecast that I have personally experienced and seen other entrepreneurs experience:

1. Create the view through the financial windshield of your business.
2. Develop a deeper understanding of your business model.
3. Strengthen your leadership muscles.
4. Help you stop doing things that lose money.
5. Prevent poor financial decisions.
6. Turn financial statements into a decision-making tool.
7. Anticipate the financial implications of growing your business.
8. Tap into the power of a strategically focused CFO.
9. Transform your accounting function into a strategic asset.
10. Promote a deeper understanding of your financial statements.
11. Reduce the risk of error in your financial statements.
12. Reveal answers to your month-to-month business and financial questions.
13. Create a tsunami warning system for your business.

As you read each benefit, take a minute to seriously reflect on the specifics of how that benefit can help make you and your company stronger. Imagine you have already implemented a forecasting process and it's become part of your monthly rhythm of financial management and improvement. Visualize that benefit working for you every single month in your business. Imagine your newfound sense of control and confidence over the financial side of your business.

Let's look at each benefit in more detail.

Create the view through the financial windshield of your business. The rearview mirror in an automobile is a helpful feature in keeping you safe on the road. It helps you see dangers that may be lurking behind you. In fact, we generally have three rearview mirrors (and only one windshield). It would be foolish to drive without your rearview mirrors. But you'll notice the rearview mirrors are very *small*. And the windshield is very *big*. For good reason. You need a clear view of what's in front of you to get where you are going safely. And the faster you're going the more important it is to have a clear view of the road ahead.

Financial statements are like rearview mirrors in that they provide you a number of different perspectives on what's already happened. It's interesting that executives generally think they don't have *any* financial information until they get their financial statements. They mistakenly view financial statements as the starting point for evaluating their financial results. But that's not reality. That's not how business really works. It doesn't *start* with what happened (the view of the past). It starts with what you are trying to make happen in the business (the view of the near future).

The financial statements become valuable when you look at what actually happened and compare that to your goals and expectations. Financial statements are step two in driving performance. Step one is a clear view through the financial windshield of your business (a reliable financial forecast).

Develop a deeper understanding of your business model. One of the first things you will notice in the forecasting process is that it is a top-down rather a bottom-up exercise. It is very different than the approach to preparing historical financial statements. Creating historical financial statements is a process of gathering and recording individual transactions in a general ledger. It is a bottom-up, accumulation process. The financial statements then summarize the accumulation of all those transactions.

On the other hand, a forecast estimates future results largely by identifying the three to five key drivers of financial performance.

This is an eye-opening exercise because it forces you to hone in on what really makes your business tick financially.

Let's say you are forecasting monthly sales. Think for a minute at a very summary level while you look at the sales number on your income statement. What two numbers could you multiply together to arrive at sales?

- For a retailer it might be number of customers x average ticket = sales.
- For a law firm it might be hours incurred by attorneys x average billing rate = sales.
- For a wholesaler of fuel it might be gallons of fuel sold x average selling price per gallon = sales.

This exercise allows you to rise up to the 30,000-foot level and look at your business from above. One of the first things you will notice is that the key drivers almost always include nonfinancial data (like number of customers in the retail example, hours worked in the law firm example, and gallons sold in the fuel wholesaler example). Some of the most important assumptions you make in a financial forecast are those related to the *nonfinancial* components of your business. You will be surprised what you learn as you hone in on the key nonfinancial drivers of performance.

The process of looking at the big picture and *simplifying* it to its essence is incredibly insightful. It moves you to search for the "levers" in your business that can really move the needle financially. You will discover a number of unexpected "aha" moments along the way.

In addition, as you get further along in creating your financial forecast and you begin making specific assumptions about financial performance, you have to constantly ask yourself whether you can really achieve the financial results you are forecasting. "Can we really add new customers at the rate I am projecting over the next twelve months? How much will we have to increase operating expenses in order to expand our presence into the Southwest? How fast can a new salesperson start bringing on new sales in order to cover their salary and overhead costs?"

The process forces you to look hard for any weak links in your growth strategy. You have to evaluate the likelihood of being able to actually execute and deliver the results you are forecasting. You will discover some powerful insights about your business model as you become more intimately familiar with what really drives financial performance in your business and where the real levers of financial performance are hiding.

Strengthen your leadership muscles. Leadership is about taking a company on a journey and building a team that understands your vision and signs on to the work and commitment required to create success. The best leaders do a fantastic job of communicating their vision for the company and attracting the talent that can help turn their vision into reality. It requires that you persistently and consistently talk about the vision you have for the company. Always helping people both inside the company and outside the company to more clearly identify with your goals and what success looks like to you.

Financial forecasting is the ideal tool to help you paint a picture of what your vision and goals look like *financially*. It helps you lead people in the direction you want the company to go financially. The forecasting process is about hooking your vision and strategy for your company up to the likely financial implications of achieving that strategy. It forces you to think about your company, and communicate your vision, in a different way. It exercises your "leadership muscles" because it helps you link your vision to a range of likely financial outcomes. It helps you put some "guardrails" around what you think should happen financially. It helps you communicate your vision in a more concrete way.

This is especially helpful if you are trying to raise capital or attract a lender. Financially minded professionals love a great vision…

together with a well-thought-out path for how that vision translates into financial results (money).

Help you stop doing things that lose money. I learned an important lesson early in my career:

The fastest way to make more money in business is to stop doing things that lose money.

I've seen too many money-losing initiatives stay alive far too long because someone high up the leadership chain had a special connection to the project. It pains them to admit defeat and make serious changes or kill the money-draining activities all together. Their hope that improvement is just around the corner clouds their view of reality.

So I talk to them about their optimism or expectations and turn that into a financial forecast. Now I've created an accountability tool to compare actual results to forecast results as each month goes by. Reality begins to set in when they see in black and white that actual results and expected results are consistently miles apart from each other. I've found this to be a very effective way to help the leadership team make decisions that almost instantly improve profits and cash flow.

Prevent poor financial decisions. A forecast can be the ideal tool for heading off poor decisions in advance. Have you ever had an executive or someone in your company that had grand plans for a new venture or a new project and you were almost certain it was going to lose money? But you didn't want to be the one person that was always being perceived as overly pessimistic or always shooting down new ideas?

My experience is that encouraging (and assisting) that person in creating a forecast helps to shine a light on the key assumptions behind their optimism. Sometimes it becomes obvious on the surface that the assumptions are way out of line with reality. Sometimes that's all it takes to bring a dose of logic and realism to the discussion. Other times the assumptions are not so far out of line and the planning focuses on additional actions or strategies to help make the project a success. It brings the people involved in the venture into the process of creating meaningful assumptions. Then comparing actual results to the forecast helps ensure everyone has a good view of what's working and what's not working once a project is approved and implemented. With a reliable financial forecast, you can provide actual results against the forecast every month. It is an incredibly effective way to create accountability around new projects or ventures.

Turn financial statements into a decision-making tool. Financial information becomes powerful when it's simple and easy to digest, understand, and act on. You want your financial information to be viewed as a fantastic, can't live without it, decision-making tool in your company. You want information about what has happened and what's about to happen to be action-oriented. You want a crystal clear link in each manager's mind between what they set out to achieve, what actually happened, and what's about to happen. That way they can quickly and easily see what they need to do (or change) in order to get the results they are responsible to achieve going forward.

It's about turning numbers into insight and action.

Anticipate the financial implications of growing your business. Depending on the industry and your company's business model, rapid growth is almost always a net user of cash in the early days of growth. Many executives are caught by surprise when they are successful in growing their company only to grow their way right into a cash crisis. They end up running to the bank and begging on bended knee for a line of credit or an increase on their existing line of credit. That hurts your credibility.

> "Growth sucks cash – the first law of entrepreneurial gravity.
>
> Yet many growth company leaders pay more attention to revenue and profit than they do to cash when it comes to structuring deals with suppliers, customers, employees (think bonus plans), or investors/banks."
>
> —Verne Harnish, *Scaling Up*

Imagine you have an aggressive plan for expanding your business into a new territory or a new customer segment. You can feel the adrenaline kick in as you get your team fired up to implement the plan. If this works, you could easily double or triple revenues and create a new level of momentum and success within your company. But you know it won't be easy. In fact, your own management team is a bit skeptical. Even your trusted advisors outside the company have pointed out that your plan seems overly aggressive. They have said things like "Are you sure you can hit such aggressive growth targets? What happens if it doesn't work? Maybe you should slow down a bit."

Despite their concerns, you press on because you are confident you can make it happen. You get some early wins and now you are "cooking with gas." Customers love you. They're referring you to prospects so fast that you're thinking about reducing your marketing budget. Revenues are growing even faster than your aggressive plans called for. Profitability is climbing faster as well.

There's just one problem. *You're running out of cash.* The accounting department is dragging its feet on payments to vendors to make sure it can cover payroll. A financial tension is building within the company that doesn't feel right. You're asking yourself, "Why is cash so tight when our growth plan is firing on all cylinders?"

Here's what happened:

- Getting that new office up and running used cash in the form of capital expenditures (which were recorded on the balance sheet as assets rather than expenses in the P&L).
- Hiring people in advance of winning new customers used cash in the early months of the plan.
- The new customers you landed are accustomed to sixty-day payment terms, which is more than double what you extend to existing customers. Accounts receivable are growing fast.
- Your business sells products and it's very important to deliver the product to your new customers immediately after they order. That means you have to have the inventory on hand in advance of getting the customer order. Your inventory levels have doubled over the last six months.

Most of your cash is still working its way through the "order to cash" cycle. A large portion of the growth you have achieved is tied up in the assets that are supporting that growth. Capital expenditures are up (to create the physical presence in the new territory/market). Accounts receivable is up (much of the increase in revenues has not yet been turned into cash). Inventory is up (more cash is tied up in the products you plan to sell to new customers). A big portion of your cash is sitting in those assets.

The irony is you are now looking weak to lenders and investors even though you accomplished what you set out to do in your aggressive growth plan. You hit a homerun. But now you have to deal with the big credibility hit you are taking because you are trying desperately to find cash.

A reliable forecast would have painted a picture of this cash scenario long before you began implementing your growth plan. You could have reviewed different avenues for handling the cash implications of achieving your growth plan. Maybe putting a bank line of credit in place in advance would have been a great way to handle the increased accounts receivable and inventory. Maybe shareholders would have been willing to fund the short-term impact on cash. Maybe you would have decided to execute your plan in smaller increments so you could fund the cash implications internally. The key is you could have been proactive rather than reactive. You could have taken the steps that were necessary and prudent long before you actually needed the cash. And your credibility and reputation with lenders and others would not have been tarnished in the process.

Tap into the power of a strategically focused CFO. The challenge many CFOs and controllers face today is that they are too often seen as the "historian" in the company—a person focused exclusively on what happened in the past (and sometimes overly focused on control and compliance). Financial forecasting changes that by transforming your CFO into a value-adding rock star.

One of the beauties of the forecasting process is it forces your CFO (or the person helping you in the forecasting process) to talk about and understand the vision and strategy of the company. They have to think through the likely financial implications of achieving that vision and strategy. They have to understand how the goals and initiatives being implemented day-to-day will impact financial results. As they bring that information together, they can begin helping you and your management team see not only what happened in the past, but what's about to happen in the near future.

As their understanding of the strategy grows, the conversations they have with you and your leadership team begins to change. They're talking about the larger strategy and goals of the company more often. They become a more important part of the overall planning process. It helps them add value and make your company stronger at the same time.

Transform your accounting function into a strategic asset. The accounting department in many companies today is viewed strictly as a cost center—an overhead drain that hurts profitability (oftentimes for good reason). Most accounting departments are not perceived as a source of strategic value inside the company. Part of the challenge is that much of the traditional work in accounting has to do with:

- Gathering and recording transactions
- Setting policies
- Defining processes
- Enforcing controls
- Safeguarding assets
- Creating financial statements
- Preparing and filing tax returns

The larger problem is that accountants are taught that their primary mission is to gather and record transactions in order to create historical financial statements. The historical financial statements show actual results for a specific period and present the financial position at a specific point in time (both of which are in the past). No doubt that's an important part of the role of CFO. But as a person leading a business, you are trying to *make something happen*. You have a plan for what you want the business to accomplish. You're starting with *expected* financial results, *not* actual financial results. Historical financial information only becomes insightful when you can clearly see how actual results compare to expected results.

Forecasting provides an opportunity for your accounting function to add value in a unique and memorable way that goes past the traditional role of accounting. You can move your accounting function away from the old perception of being a necessary evil or merely a cost center in the business. You can show that it's a part of the team dedicated to winning in business and helping make your company stronger. As you do that you are also improving the professional lives of everyone in the accounting department. You are showing them their work can be done in a way that adds value and builds relationships with people in other parts of the business.

Promote a deeper understanding of your financial statements. As you begin the forecasting process, you begin to think more deeply about what drives financial performance in your company. You begin to think about the impact each of those drivers has on revenues, expenses, and ultimately on the cash you have access to. You begin to better understand what causes your financial statements to change from month to month. Once the actual financial statements come out each month, you look to see if the financial results are in line with what you forecast them to be. When there are differences between actual and forecast results, you "peel the onion" to find out why. The financial statements begin to make better sense. Your management team better understands how their actions and initiatives impact the financial statements. Now everyone can begin using the financial statements to make better decisions throughout the business.

Reduce the risk of error in your financial statements. Here is a benefit of forecasting that few entrepreneurs or CFOs realize or take advantage of. Having an expectation of what the financial statements should look like at the end of any month helps catch errors or unusual results in your monthly review of financial statements. A CFO should have an expectation of what the financials should look like long before receiving the first draft to review after month-end. The first review of the financials should be a top-down review based on what you expect them to look like.

I used to surprise my staff because they would bring me the financials they had been working so hard on, which included thousands of transactions across twenty companies rolled up into a nice income statement, balance sheet, and cash flows, and I could hone in on a number that seemed out of whack in a matter of minutes. I had already put the thought into what was likely to happen financially when I created the forecast. So I had a reliable expectation of what the financial statements should look like without needing to drill down into every detail. I could "sniff out" problems in short order.

In addition, you will notice a very interesting thing starts to happen as you begin providing the forward looking view of financial performance. The historical financials become even *more* important to you and your management team. You begin paying *more* attention to the financial statements. Once you have a good view of what to expect financially, you want to see how things actually turn out each month.

Everyone begins paying closer attention to the financial statements which further reduces the likelihood of error or fraud in a significant way.

Reveal answers to your month-to-month financial questions. When you have basic questions about the business running around in your head, but you are unsure of what the answers are, you are either going to make some bad decisions or have a vague sense of confusion or uncertainty in the back of your mind. You don't want that. You want clarity and confidence so questions can be considered in the open and reviewed in the context of their likely financial implications.

Questions a Retailer Might Have

- Can I add another location?
- Can I hire a new Sales VP?
- Can I pay our debt back on time?
- Will I have enough cash to get through the slow months?
- Can I buy the new equipment I need?

Questions a Professional Services Firm Might Have

- Will we have enough cash to pay year-end bonuses?
- How much can the partners take out this year?
- Do we have enough cash for payroll in two weeks?
- How much do we need to bill to hit our revenue targets?

Questions a Public Company Might Have

- What will EPS (earnings per share) be this year?
- What will the balance on the line of credit be at the end of the year?
- Is there any risk of busting a debt covenant?
- How do our growth targets compare to our peers?

These are the kinds of questions you need insight and answers to day-to-day. A reliable financial forecast helps provide the answers. A forecast also provides a wake-up call when it looks like the company may miss on important financial measures or expectations.

Create a tsunami warning system for your business. If you are on a beautiful island enjoying a white sand beach and crystal blue water and there is an earthquake thousands of miles away in the ocean, you need a tsunami warning system to alert you that a huge wall of water may be headed your way.

Do you remember the terrible tsunami that struck Asia back in 2004? It was a tragedy where as many as 280,000 people died.

A magnitude 9.1 earthquake occurred in the Indian Ocean, 100 miles off the western coast of Northern Sumatra. Within hours, the massive waves generated by the earthquake created enormous devastation in many countries.

One of the discussions after that tragedy was the lack of a tsunami warning system in the Indian Ocean. A tsunami warning system can detect the wave, or predict the magnitude of the wave based on the information about the earthquake, and then provide warnings to all the places where the tsunami is expected to impact. But there was no warning system in place in 2004 and a tragedy ensued as a result.

There is an analogy here that can help you. Say you're in a cabin just 20 feet or so from the ocean. Suddenly a huge 50-foot wave crashes onto the beach. Water starts roaring through the doors and windows of the cabin. What will you start doing immediately and instinctively?

- Hold on for dear life.
- Try to keep your head above water.
- Try to find something to grab onto so you can pull yourself to safety.
- Try to avoid being hit by chunks of debris racing past you in the water.

That's the basic picture of what you might be doing when a crisis hits you without warning. Now let's look at a different scenario. You're in a beautiful cabin just 20 feet or so from the ocean. Suddenly you receive a tsunami warning. It's telling you an earthquake has happened, and a huge wave is headed your way and it could be there within hours.

What will you start doing right away?

- Get your children rounded up real fast.
- Get anyone else in the house rounded up.
- Maybe grab a few precious possessions or heirlooms.

- Throw some clothes or food in a bag.
- Get the family in the car and start driving away from the ocean.
- Turn on the radio and check your smartphone to learn what's going on and get traffic reports.

In both scenarios you are moving fast and everything you are doing is important. But *what* you are doing is very different. In one case you're fighting just to stay alive. In the other, you're protecting your loved ones, saving your keepsakes and valuables, and moving to a safer place. You're avoiding the problem. *What* you're doing and *when* you are doing it are very, very different because you received a warning that a problem was on its way. You knew what kind of problem it was, how big a problem it was, and when it was expected to happen. You had the information you needed to take action.

A reliable financial forecast is a tsunami warning system for your business.

A reliable forecast provides the "heads up" you need when a financial problem is brewing. It gives you time to figure out a solution or find ways to minimize the potential negative impact. It helps you see financial problems or challenges in advance—far enough in advance for you to develop and implement an action plan to solve the problems before they arrive on your doorstep.

The Pledge

Here's a powerful way for you to get started. The Pledge is a cool concept in a book titled, well, *The Pledge* by Michael Masterson.

Just for fun, I'd like you to consider putting the spirit of the pledge to work in your business. How? By making a simple commitment to yourself and to me. Ready?

Okay, Philip. I am with you. I am absolutely committed to driving my business to new levels of financial success. My business is very important to me and I plan to do everything in my power to ensure it survives and thrives financially. As I read your book, I promise to seriously consider making financial forecasting a key part of how I manage my business every month and how I drive growth, profitability, and cash flow higher and higher over time.

Name   _____

Date   _____

PART TWO

How to Plan, Create, and Present Your Forecast

"Most senior executives (not all) either come out of finance or pick up the skills during their rise to the top, just because it's tough to run a business unless you know what the financial folks are saying."

—*Karen Berman and Joe Knight with John Case,* Financial Intelligence

Chapter 3

10 Rules for Creating a Forecast You Can Trust

"The few things that work fantastically well should be identified, cultivated, nurtured, and multiplied."

—Richard Koch, *The 80/20 Principle*

The 10 rules I walk through in this chapter are incredibly important as you get started in forecasting. They form the foundation you will need to make sure you get started on the right foot. Please spend a few extra minutes to read (and re-read) each one. Put some serious thought into each rule. I promise you that the extra time you spend with these rules, or principles, will pay dividends and ensure you create a forecasting process you can trust.

1. It's all about decision making, not precision
2. Think top-down, not bottom-up
3. Model a full set of financial statements
4. First look back, then look forward
5. Understand the high-level company strategy and expectations
6. Simplify, simplify, simplify

7. Create a repeatable process

8. Be conservative

9. Condense the results to a 2-minute summary

10. Start for your eyes only

Let's look at each one.

Rule #1. It's All About Decision Making, Not Precision

One thing that may be stopping you from creating a forecast is that little voice in your head saying, "But I don't know exactly what the future holds—what if I'm wrong in my forecast?" That fear of being wrong is rooted in the mistaken idea that a forecast should be "accurate."

Transaction processing and creating historical financial statements is about being right. (Here, precision is your friend.) On the other hand, forecasting is about improving the company's ability to make wise decisions. (Here, precision is your enemy.)

Here is an example. Let's say at the beginning of the year you told your bank and outside investors that your plan was to increase pre-tax income to $1.1 million this year and reduce debt by $750,000. Results for the first half of the year had come in better than budget and you were feeling confident. Now it's mid-year and you are updating your monthly forecast for the remainder of the year.

From a decision-making perspective, the question is whether the company has a good shot at hitting the full year pre-tax income and debt reduction targets or not. If the company is likely to hit the targets, then your management team's focus should be on continuing to execute the existing plan. If the targets are in jeopardy, then you and your team need to evaluate what's not working and make changes now to get back on track to hit the financial targets.

After you review the forecast it becomes clear that the last half of the year is likely to come in far below the first half. Figure 3-1 is a summary of the resulting forecast compared to last year and the plan for this year.

Figure 3-1
FORECAST SUMMARY

(Amounts in Thousands)

	Last Year (Actual)	This Year (Plan)	This Year (Forecast)
Revenues	$6,250	$7,500	$7,000
Gross margin	23.4%	24.0%	23.0%
Pre-tax income	**$813**	**$1,125**	**$800**
Cash	$875	$1,000	$500
Accounts receivable	$1,113	$1,000	$1,300
Distributions to owners	$325	$450	$600
Debt	**$2,500**	**$1,750**	**$2,500**

Is a forecast always right? No. Is pre-tax income likely to come in at precisely $800,000? No.

From a precision perspective, lots of questions will arise such as what will actual revenues and expenses turn out to be, which of your current prospects will turn into actual customers, will there be employee turnover that could disrupt the business, will a specific customer pay their invoice by the due date, and a host of other detailed questions that you would need to know to arrive at a precise estimate of pre-tax income and cash available for debt reduction.

But what is very clear in the forecast is there is a substantial risk of missing the pre-tax income and debt reduction targets for the year. It is crystal clear based on the forecast that management attention is required in order to get the company back on track for the last half of the year.

Chasing precision will only serve to cloud the message and distract from the important work of getting the company back on track to meeting its financial goals.

"Debating 'what is the right number' is a waste of management time. Instead, the focus should be on 'what is the range of possible outcomes.'"

—Steve Morlidge and Steve Player, *Future Ready: How to Master Business Forecasting*

RULE #2. THINK TOP-DOWN, NOT BOTTOM-UP

Although creating historical financial statements is a bottom-up process of gathering and recording thousands of transactions and reporting the results in the form of accurate financial statements, creating a financial forecast is a top-down exercise. You are connecting the company's vision and strategy to the likely financial implications of achieving that strategy.

Forecasting uses big-picture drivers and assumptions to create a model of what the financial statements may look like based on existing trends and plans. You have to take yourself up to the 30,000-foot level and look down on the business financially as you forecast. It's about painting a picture of what the financial results will likely be based on your knowledge and intuition rather than actual transactions. Your forecast looks at the strategic view and direction of where the company is going—not the nitty-gritty bottom-up details.

Consider the many assumptions that go into creating a fully modeled set of financial statements. In the income statement, you forecast revenues, cost of sales, operating expenses, and net income. On the balance sheet, you forecast monthly balances for cash, accounts receivable, inventory, property and equipment, accounts payable, accrued liabilities, debt, and equity balances. A bottom-up approach to create those assumptions is overly complex and counterproductive.

Thinking top-down will help you resist the temptation to drive your estimates and assumptions down to the lowest level.

RULE #3. MODEL A FULL SET OF FINANCIAL STATEMENTS

A reliable financial forecast is a living, breathing tool that is updated monthly. The basic format should track with your existing financial statements (income statement, balance sheet, and statement of cash flows in the same format you use for monthly financial reporting) for at least the next six to eighteen months. Figures 3-2 through 3-4 show a full set of monthly financial statements as an example. We'll talk more about ABC Construction Company as a real world forecasting example in Chapter 5.

RULE #4. FIRST LOOK BACK, THEN LOOK FORWARD

One of the biggest mistakes entrepreneurs (and CFOs) make in creating a forecast is to start with a clean slate. They pull up a blank spreadsheet and begin thinking about what the first month in the forecast will look like. The problem is you unhook your forecast from reality when you do that.

The first step should be to drop in actual results for the last six to eighteen months (or more). Have the revenues and expenses been coming in the way you expected them to? Can you see a trend developing? Are you surprised by any of the numbers now that you are looking at the last six to eighteen months of actual results next to each other?

Once you have a good view of what the financial results have been over the last six to eighteen months, you want to look at some of the

Figure 3-2: INCOME STATEMENTS – Prior Year

ABC Construction Company	Actual Jan	Actual Feb	Actual Mar	Actual Apr	Actual May	Actual Jun	Actual Jul	Actual Aug	Actual Sep	Actual Oct	Actual Nov	Actual Dec	Actual Year
Number of projects	15	16	14	15	15	17	19	19	15	14	15	15	15
Average revenue per project	$129,550	$133,599	$155,738	$115,181	$132,477	$128,581	$109,294	$130,551	$143,284	$135,096	$119,785	$99,108	$1,602,864
Revenues	$1,943,256	$2,137,582	$2,180,333	$1,727,710	$1,987,156	$2,185,871	$2,076,578	$2,480,467	$2,149,258	$1,891,347	$1,796,780	$1,486,619	$24,042,956
Total	1,943,256	2,137,582	2,180,333	1,727,710	1,987,156	2,185,871	2,076,578	2,480,467	2,149,258	1,891,347	1,796,780	1,486,619	24,042,956
Cost of good sold	1,663,427	1,791,293	1,855,464	1,489,286	1,683,121	1,840,504	1,731,866	2,120,799	1,818,272	1,647,363	1,520,076	1,250,246	20,411,717
Gross profit	279,829	346,288	324,870	238,424	304,035	345,368	344,712	359,668	330,986	243,984	276,704	236,372	3,631,239
	14.4%	16.2%	14.9%	13.8%	15.3%	15.8%	16.6%	14.5%	15.4%	12.9%	15.4%	15.9%	15.1%
OPERATING EXPENSES													
Employee wages & taxes	101,467	104,638	121,978	110,638	127,252	112,612	110,490	111,441	116,897	116,870	103,625	110,690	1,348,598
Rent	14,750	14,820	14,760	15,357	17,663	14,800	14,800	14,800	14,800	14,800	14,800	14,800	180,950
Advertising & marketing	5,328	5,495	6,405	4,737	5,448	5,288	4,495	5,369	5,893	5,556	4,926	4,076	63,016
Insurance	12,480	12,870	15,003	11,096	12,762	12,387	10,529	12,576	13,803	13,014	11,539	9,547	147,606
Telephone & utilities	3,544	3,655	4,260	3,151	3,624	3,517	2,990	3,571	3,920	3,696	3,277	2,711	41,916
Travel, meals & entertainment	2,853	2,942	3,430	2,537	2,917	2,832	2,407	2,875	3,155	2,975	2,638	2,183	33,744
Professional fees	4,500	4,641	5,410	4,001	4,602	4,466	3,796	4,535	4,977	4,693	4,161	3,443	53,223
Office expenses	2,980	3,073	3,582	2,649	3,047	2,958	2,514	3,003	3,296	3,108	2,755	2,280	35,246
Depreciation & amortization	5,475	5,475	5,475	5,475	5,475	5,475	5,475	5,475	5,475	5,475	5,475	10,350	70,575
All other	5,496	5,668	6,607	4,886	5,620	5,455	4,637	5,538	6,079	5,731	5,082	4,205	65,003
Total	158,873	163,276	186,910	164,527	188,411	169,790	162,132	169,184	178,295	175,918	158,278	164,284	2,039,877
Operating income	120,956	183,012	137,960	73,897	115,624	175,578	182,580	190,484	152,691	68,066	118,426	72,088	1,591,362
Interest expense	8,237	8,162	8,087	8,012	7,937	7,862	7,787	7,712	7,637	7,562	7,487	7,412	93,900
Other expense (income)	0	0	0	0	0	0	0	0	0	0	0	0	0
Total	8,237	8,162	8,087	8,012	7,937	7,862	7,787	7,712	7,637	7,562	7,487	7,412	93,900
Pretax income	$112,718	$174,850	$129,872	$65,885	$107,686	$167,716	$174,792	$182,771	$145,054	$60,504	$110,938	$64,676	$1,497,462
As % of revenues	5.8%	8.2%	6.0%	3.8%	5.4%	7.7%	8.4%	7.4%	6.7%	3.2%	6.2%	4.4%	6.2%
EBITDA	126,431	188,487	143,435	79,372	121,099	181,053	188,055	195,959	158,166	73,541	123,901	82,438	1,661,937

Figure 3-3: BALANCE SHEETS – Prior Year

ABC Construction Company	Actual Jan	Actual Feb	Actual Mar	Actual Apr	Actual May	Actual Jun	Actual Jul	Actual Aug	Actual Sep	Actual Oct	Actual Nov	Actual Dec
ASSETS												
Cash	$1,143,471	$1,340,165	$1,381,504	$1,024,989	$1,234,820	$1,445,426	$1,515,779	$2,053,095	$1,763,674	$1,470,734	$1,439,566	$826,313
Accounts receivable	2,946,231	2,924,855	2,968,462	2,916,631	2,876,887	2,920,605	2,858,308	2,932,722	2,975,707	3,013,534	2,959,630	2,915,032
Inventory	163,581	181,494	144,385	189,063	222,726	185,916	237,872	174,248	137,882	104,935	150,537	188,045
Costs & estimated earnings in excess of billings on uncompleted contracts	209,134	132,807	162,429	248,684	193,571	236,761	219,316	162,362	142,879	216,396	217,033	245,177
Other current assets	24,876	25,876	25,876	25,876	25,876	25,876	25,876	23,376	23,376	23,376	23,376	23,376
Total current assets	4,487,293	4,605,197	4,682,656	4,405,243	4,553,880	4,814,584	4,857,149	5,345,802	5,043,518	4,828,975	4,790,142	4,197,942
Machinery & equipment	202,333	202,333	217,878	217,878	221,468	221,468	221,468	245,457	245,457	249,927	249,927	249,927
Furniture, fixtures & equipment	251,590	251,590	251,590	251,590	251,590	251,590	251,590	251,590	251,590	251,590	251,590	251,590
Gross property	453,923	453,923	469,468	469,468	473,058	473,058	473,058	497,047	497,047	501,517	501,517	501,517
Less: accumulated depreciation	(150,000)	(155,475)	(160,950)	(166,425)	(171,900)	(177,375)	(182,850)	(188,325)	(193,800)	(199,275)	(204,750)	(215,100)
Net property	303,923	298,448	308,518	303,043	301,158	295,683	290,208	308,722	303,247	302,242	296,767	286,417
Total Assets	$4,791,216	$4,903,645	$4,991,174	$4,708,287	$4,855,038	$5,110,267	$5,147,358	$5,654,524	$5,346,765	$5,131,217	$5,086,910	$4,484,359
LIABILITIES & EQUITY												
Accounts payable & accrued liabilities	$1,684,389	$1,813,867	$1,878,845	$1,508,053	$1,704,331	$1,863,697	$1,753,690	$2,147,525	$1,841,185	$1,668,123	$1,539,231	$1,266,001
Short-term notes payable	478,250	468,250	458,250	448,250	438,250	428,250	418,250	408,250	398,250	388,250	378,250	368,250
Billings in excess of costs & estimated earnings on uncompleted contracts	679,321	577,423	560,100	672,120	604,908	623,055	685,361	705,922	649,448	636,459	700,105	721,108
Total current liabilities	2,841,960	2,859,539	2,897,196	2,628,424	2,747,489	2,915,002	2,857,301	3,261,697	2,888,883	2,692,832	2,617,586	2,355,360
Notes payable	1,169,245	1,164,245	1,159,245	1,154,245	1,149,245	1,144,245	1,139,245	1,134,245	1,129,245	1,124,245	1,119,245	1,114,245
Owner's investment	500,000	500,000	500,000	500,000	500,000	500,000	500,000	500,000	500,000	500,000	500,000	500,000
Owner distributions	(570,000)	(645,000)	(720,000)	(795,000)	(870,000)	(945,000)	(1,020,000)	(1,095,000)	(1,170,000)	(1,245,000)	(1,320,000)	(1,720,000)
Retained earnings	850,011	1,024,861	1,154,733	1,220,618	1,328,304	1,496,020	1,670,812	1,853,583	1,998,637	2,059,140	2,170,079	2,234,755
Total equity	780,011	879,861	934,733	925,618	958,304	1,051,020	1,150,812	1,258,583	1,328,637	1,314,140	1,350,079	1,014,755
Total liabilities & equity	$4,791,216	$4,903,645	$4,991,174	$4,708,287	$4,855,038	$5,110,267	$5,147,358	$5,654,524	$5,346,765	$5,131,217	$5,086,910	$4,484,359

Figure 3-4: **STATEMENTS OF CASH FLOWS – Prior Year**

ABC Construction Company	Actual Jan	Actual Feb	Actual Mar	Actual Apr	Actual May	Actual Jun	Actual Jul	Actual Aug	Actual Sep	Actual Oct	Actual Nov	Actual Dec	Actual Year
Pre-tax income	$112,718	$174,850	$129,872	$65,885	$107,686	$167,716	$174,792	$182,771	$145,054	$60,504	$110,938	$64,676	$1,497,462
Depreciation and amortization	5,475	5,475	5,475	5,475	5,475	5,475	5,475	5,475	5,475	5,475	5,475	10,350	70,575
Decrease (increase) in accounts receivable	(15,679)	21,376	(43,607)	51,831	39,743	(43,717)	62,297	(74,414)	(42,985)	(37,827)	53,903	44,599	15,520
Decrease (increase) in inventory	3,425	(17,913)	37,109	(44,679)	(33,662)	36,810	(51,956)	63,624	36,365	32,947	(45,602)	(37,507)	(21,039)
Decrease (increase) in costs & estimated earnings in excess of billings on uncompleted contracts	(11,745)	76,327	(29,622)	(86,255)	55,114	(43,190)	17,446	56,953	19,483	(73,518)	(636)	(28,144)	(47,788)
Decrease (increase) in other current assets	1,250	(1,000)	0	0	0	0	0	2,500	0	0	0	0	2,750
(Decrease) increase in accounts payable & accrued liabilities	(18,902)	129,478	64,979	(370,792)	196,278	159,366	(110,007)	393,835	(306,339)	(173,063)	(128,892)	(273,230)	(437,290)
(Decrease) increase in short-term notes payable	(10,000)	(10,000)	(10,000)	(10,000)	(10,000)	(10,000)	(10,000)	(10,000)	(10,000)	(10,000)	(10,000)	(10,000)	(120,000)
(Decrease) increase in billings in excess of costs & estimated earnings on uncompleted contracts	35,024	(101,898)	(17,323)	112,020	(67,212)	18,147	62,306	20,561	(56,474)	(12,989)	63,646	21,003	76,812
Net cash provided by operating activities	101,566	276,694	136,884	(276,515)	293,421	290,606	150,353	641,305	(209,421)	(208,470)	48,832	(208,254)	1,037,003
CASH FLOWS - INVESTING ACTIVITIES													
Purchase of property and equipment	(23,540)	0	(15,545)	0	(3,590)	0	0	(23,989)	0	(4,470)	0	0	(71,134)
Net cash provided (used) by investing activities	(23,540)	0	(15,545)	0	(3,590)	0	0	(23,989)	0	(4,470)	0	0	(71,134)
CASH FLOWS - FINANCING ACTIVITIES													
Payments on long-term debt	(5,000)	(5,000)	(5,000)	(5,000)	(5,000)	(5,000)	(5,000)	(5,000)	(5,000)	(5,000)	(5,000)	(5,000)	(60,000)
Distributions to owners	(175,000)	(75,000)	(75,000)	(75,000)	(75,000)	(75,000)	(75,000)	(75,000)	(75,000)	(75,000)	(75,000)	(400,000)	(1,325,000)
Net cash provided (used) by financiang activities	(180,000)	(80,000)	(80,000)	(80,000)	(80,000)	(80,000)	(80,000)	(80,000)	(80,000)	(80,000)	(80,000)	(405,000)	(1,385,000)
Increase (decrease) in cash	(101,974)	196,694	41,339	(356,515)	209,831	210,606	70,353	537,316	(289,421)	(292,940)	(31,168)	(613,254)	(419,131)
Cash at beginning of month	1,245,444	1,143,471	1,340,165	1,381,504	1,024,989	1,234,820	1,445,426	1,515,779	2,053,095	1,763,674	1,470,734	1,439,566	1,245,444
Cash at end of month	$1,143,471	$1,340,165	$1,381,504	$1,024,989	$1,234,820	$1,445,426	$1,515,779	$2,053,095	$1,763,674	$1,470,734	$1,439,566	$826,313	$826,313

factors that can make the next six to eighteen months vary from the historical results. That could include things like seasonality, a change in service or product mix, whether you will be expanding geographically, etc.

For example, if you owned a construction company, you would first review your most recent financial results to see trends in the number of existing projects, gross margins, working capital, and capital expenditures. Then you would consider what kinds of bids are outstanding. Are they targeted at construction projects similar to those in the past? Are they for smaller or larger projects? Are the gross margins consistent with current projects, or are they higher or lower? A construction company owner would want to think through the way the business is changing and the impact it's likely to have on financial results and cash flow. They would talk to project managers and others about what they are seeing in the market. Does customer activity seem to be picking up or slowing down? Management and others inside the company are a wealth of information that will shed light on what's changing and what's about to happen as a result.

Here is another example. I use a forecasting tool called SurvivalWare which I will talk more about shortly. It is a powerful tool for financial analysis and forecasting that I have used for well over ten years now. The really cool thing in SurvivalWare is we push a button to see a graph and now we have our forecast amounts next to actuals in a bar chart. Figure 3-5 is a great example of a forecast that has an obvious problem.

There are actually two problems with this forecast. First, sales go up almost $4 million in the first month of the forecast. Second, the projection shows sales going up consistently each month. But that trend is not at all consistent with the recent past. The actual results show that there is seasonality to the business. And you can bet that the seasonality of the business will not just magically disappear.

So I used the forecast tool in SurvivalWare to include the seasonality in the actuals in the projected sales levels. Figure 3-6 shows the result.

Figure 3-5
SALES: ACTUAL & FORECAST

(Without Seasonality)

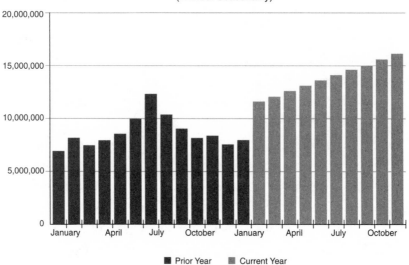

Figure 3-6
SALES: ACTUAL & FORECAST

(With Seasonality)

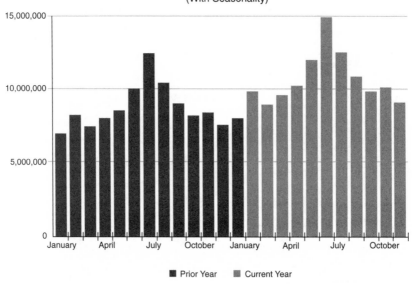

This is a much more reality-based view of the fact that sales bounce around a bit. I still have a sales increase in the forecast, but now it reflects the obvious seasonality of this business. You want to do this kind of review on each of the key line items in your forecast.

Rule #5. Understand the High-Level Company Strategy and Expectations

One of the benefits of forecasting is that it forces you to think about your company's vision and strategy more deeply. For example, what are the three most critical goals or initiatives for the coming year? Is the company planning to grow slowly or aggressively? Are there plans to move into new markets or attempt to attract new customer segments? Answering these types of strategic questions forces you to step back and think about the big picture. If you have a CFO it helps him or her "get out of the ledger" and talk to management about their division's goals or their department's strategies. It requires you to talk to your board and trusted advisors to get their input and perspective.

One thing I always do when I help a company put a reliable financial forecasting process in place is to surface the expectations of the CEO, the board, and others. I love to get a view of what they expect to happen financially in the business. Then I share with them what the forecast results reveal about what financial performance is likely to be and compare it to their expectations. It would shock you how often the reality and the expectations differ.

Rule #6. Simplify, Simplify, Simplify

One of my favorite quotes, known as Meyer's Law, says:

> "It's a simple matter to make things complex, but a complex matter to make things simple."

You will be surprised how difficult this advice is to implement once you begin creating, and regularly updating, your financial forecast. The number of potential rabbit holes you can dive into while forecasting is huge.

With all the assumptions you have to make in creating your forecast, it is very important to think about one of the more counter-intuitive facts about forecasting:

The more detail you bring into the forecasting process, the more error you will create.

I learned this very early in my career when forecasting revenues.

I was the CFO of an international franchisor. We had three retail concepts and 350 locations across the United States and Canada. We needed a reliable forecast of our combined revenues and cash flow. One of the larger obstacles was that we lacked real-time access to franchisee sales at the location level. The sales information was sent to us monthly (ten days after month end—this was in the early 1990s).

We considered having each franchisee forecast their sales and submit it to us at corporate. But that was met with resistance. Plus, there was no way we would have anywhere near full compliance with that many franchisees involved. We tried forecasting each location ourselves and summing it up for our overall forecast. But that process proved unreliable.

We tried having our regional managers provide their estimate by store because they were talking and meeting with franchisees frequently. But that proved unreliable as well and it put a lot of additional work on the regional managers.

I found the solution by estimating one number – comparable store sales increase/decrease. There was no need to estimate 350 different numbers. We only needed to estimate one number.

To get the forecast revenue number, I would review the comparable store sales change (expressed as a percentage up or down) for the last twelve months. Then I would talk to a couple regional managers to get some anecdotal feedback on whether they were hearing good things about sales or bad things. I would consider whether the revenues for the same month of the prior year were up or down. With that limited amount of information, I could estimate the comparable store sales percentage and arrive at my revenue forecast for each month.

It turned out to be amazingly reliable. Not perfect, but incredibly reliable…and dramatically simpler than the bottom-up alternative.

> "If you can't explain it simply, you don't understand it well enough."
>
> —Albert Einstein

Here's another example of the importance of simplification when you are forecasting.

An engineering company was beginning the financial forecasting process. The company began discussing how best to forecast revenues and gross profit. Most of its revenues were project related and based on a fixed price. Revenues bounced around from month to month, depending on how each project was progressing and when new projects began. It had 35 open projects, six about to start, and another five bids out. Individual projects ranged from $3,000 to $225,000, and each one was in a different phase of completion.

The company reasoned that the most accurate way to estimate revenues was to do it at the project level. Otherwise it couldn't support the forecast number. So, the company took the work in process (WIP) schedule and expanded it by adding columns for projected revenues and gross profit by month for each project over the next eighteen months. Then it added projects the company expected to start in the near future and ones it had bid on and expected to win. From there, the company created the projected revenue and gross profit for each month.

It was an impressive spreadsheet and tied nicely to the monthly revenue forecast. When the CEO or the board asked, "How did you arrive at the November revenue forecast?" they could pull up the detailed project schedule and say "Here's the revenue forecast by project."

But think about how many estimates were in that schedule: the timing and amount of possible change orders for each project, the timing and amount of changes to expected gross profit for each project, the timing and amount of cost and completion estimates for each project, the timing of new upcoming projects, the revenue and gross profit estimates for each new project, the timing of billings and monthly revenue, etc. The schedule covered 46 projects; the number of estimates for a single month of revenues was at least 108.

The challenge wasn't to answer the question: "What are the 108 different estimates we can use to arrive at a forecast of revenues for one month?" It was to figure out what *two* numbers can be multiplied to get the revenue forecast for the month. Here's the answer:

Number of open projects x Average monthly revenue per
project = Revenues

A quick look at the company's historical results showed a surprisingly consistent overall average monthly revenue per project over the past 24 months, especially considering the wide variety of projects open at any given time. And the number of open projects during each of those months did not vary widely. The two-driver forecasting approach proved that it was more reliable...and dramatically simpler.

The key to success in forecasting is to be always thinking about how to simplify, simplify, simplify...and simplify some more. Simplify the key drivers, critical assumptions, and how you interpret and present the results of the forecast.

> "...Increasing the level of detail often leads to increased forecast error.... Indeed, more often than not, more detail means higher errors, not higher accuracy."
>
> —Steve Morlidge and Steve Player, *Future Ready: How to Master Business Forecasting*

RULE #7. CREATE A REPEATABLE PROCESS

Because your forecast will be updated with actual results and the forecast adjusted every month based on current information, repeatability is very important to the forecasting process.

The software tool you choose will impact the success of your forecasting process. The tool must include the underlying logic for forecasting (modeling) a full set of financial statements and perform a number of additional functions. At a minimum, it should:

- Provide the ability to forecast with financial and nonfinancial data
- Import historical (actual) financial results
- Present both historical and forecast results in reports, report packages, and exports
- Be easy to update and maintain
- Make monthly financial reporting simple and fast
- Display graphical views of data and trends (this is a powerful feature for communicating insight)

Forecasting tools generally fall into two categories: homegrown spreadsheets and forecasting software. Creating a forecast in a spreadsheet can work well in a company with spreadsheet "power users," analysts on staff to maintain the financial model, or an organization that prefers "roll your own" solutions to acquiring software from outside vendors. Spreadsheets can be fully customized and are relatively inexpensive to get started.

However, spreadsheets are not ideal for a company in which a complex legal entity consolidation is required to present consolidated actual and forecast results, or one that is moving its system to a cloud-based solution with anytime, anywhere access to financial data. Spreadsheets can become clunky and difficult to maintain, involve a lot of manual input, and are prone to human error.

Forecasting software is specialized, dynamic, and built for mass amounts of data as well as the ability to import data and perform complex reporting. However, it can be a costly solution that requires professional assistance and extra time to set up and maintain.

We'll talk more about forecasting tools in Chapter 6.

RULE #8. BE CONSERVATIVE

Because we know a forecast will not be perfectly accurate, the challenge is keeping it in the "ballpark" as a wildly inaccurate forecast will hurt your credibility. You do that by being conservative in your key assumptions.

It's like meeting someone for lunch. You agree to meet a good friend at a restaurant at noon. You set noon as the time to meet so you will both be there at about the same time. But despite the precise time you set, you know that both of you will not show up at exactly noon. The only question is whether you will be there a little before noon or a little after noon. Will you be early or will you be late?

It's the same for your forecast. Your estimates will not be perfectly accurate. You want to err on the side of being conservative. That way the surprises are pleasant rather than unpleasant.

Let's say you are working on the profitability component of your forecast. Last year the company generated $5.5 million of net income. This year, the economy is great and the company is growing nicely. If results continue the way they have been going, profits could hit the $8.0 million mark. Being conservative in your forecast of profitability means that you assume there could be some slips or slowdowns before year end. So your forecast might guide the profit estimate down to the $7.0 million to $7.5 million range. That way you provide some room for error or surprise. It recognizes that not every "at bat" results in a home run.

RULE #9. CONDENSE THE RESULTS TO A 2-MINUTE SUMMARY

Creating a reliable forecast and effectively communicating it to your audience starts with making the forecast results simple and easy to understand. Here is a helpful exercise that works especially well when implementing a forecast process for the first time.

Imagine you will sit down with the CEO or board tomorrow morning. In that meeting, you will have two minutes to convey the essence of the forecast (key insights, implications, and assumptions) to him or her. That person will then step into another meeting with the company's key shareholders and lenders to share his or her insight about where the company is going financially. Your mission: Ensure they can share the insights from the forecast with confidence and clarity.

This exercise will force you to distill the insights and implications of the forecast down to what matters most so that you can clearly identify and communicate the most important high-level drivers and assumptions.

Here's an example:

Figure 3-7
THE 2-MINUTE SUMMARY

Based on our growth plan for the coming year, we will need to raise $1.1 million to $1.3 million in cash by June 30. The primary driver of the need to raise cash is the plan for launching a new division in Texas. The expansion is forecast at $3.0 to $3.5 million driven primarily by the capital expenditure and first-year operating losses.

In this example, there is one key insight because the expansion into Texas is a significant event. It will take about one minute to communicate that summary. The remainder of the meeting with the CEO will be spent answering his or her questions about the key assumptions and the conclusion. The number of questions the CEO has will be determined by the degree to which your conclusions or insights come as a surprise.

Rule #10. Start for Your Eyes Only

As you make progress in creating your forecast, it's natural to want to begin sharing it immediately. However, keep it "for your eyes only"—at least to start.

That means don't sell your leadership team on the value of having a forecast, don't talk to them about the assumptions or specifics as you create the forecast, and don't send the results of the forecast to them—yet.

Instead, spend a few months "beta testing" your forecast to learn from and experiment with the process before rolling it out to the management team or the board. Create assumptions at the highest level possible to prove to yourself that you don't need to forecast at the detail level. Create the forecast for the next three months, then compare the actual results each month. What worked out well? Are you surprised at the difference between your forecast and the actual results?

An important step in mitigating risk when creating a forecast is to give it a serious reality check, what I like to call a "smell test." You've created assumptions about profitability, the timing of collecting accounts receivable, inventory and payables, capital expenditures, borrowing or payments on debt, distributions to owners, and a number of other important drivers of financial results.

Once you have a completed draft of the forecast, step back and look at the resulting financial statements. Are they consistent with your general expectations? Are they in line with actual results and the plan? Do they make sense given your intuition and knowledge of the business?

One thing you learn real fast when forecasting a full set of financial statements is that the real bottom line is cash. Because every forecast assumption you make ultimately impacts the cash balance, you want to pay very close attention to the forecast cash balances to ensure nothing looks unusual. The smell test is a quick way to check that nothing unexpected has made its way into your numbers.

After running the forecast process for three months, you will become more confident and knowledgeable about the benefits of forecasting and how best to create and present the results. You will learn firsthand where the landmines are to avoid. You will develop a better sense of the kinds of monthly and strategic decisions that the forecast can help you answer and influence.

Figure 3-8

10 RULES FOR CREATING A FORECAST YOU CAN TRUST

1.	It's all about decision making, not precision
2.	Think top-down, not bottom-up
3.	Model a full set of financial statements
4.	First look back, then look forward
5.	Understand the high-level company strategy and expectations
6.	Simplify, simplify, simplify
7.	Create a repeatable process
8.	Be conservative
9.	Condense the results to a 2-minute summary
10.	Start for your eyes only

Chapter 4

The Recipe for Financial Forecasting

"Money is a terrible master but an excellent servant."

—P.T. Barnum

Most people whip out a spreadsheet and start plugging numbers into a forecast only to realize there is more to the forecasting process than meets the eye. That's why I have organized the forecasting process into three phases—plan, create, and present.

The **plan** phase is about putting the foundation in place so you can build a forecast that adds value for the company. The **create** phase is about the actual work of developing assumptions and putting numbers in the forecast. The **present** phase is about how you turn the forecast into insight for your leadership team and others interested in, or invested in, the financial success of your company.

PLAN

In this phase, you'll plan and design the ultimate end product and build a foundation that will support your forecasting goals.

Figure 4-1

THE RECIPE FOR FINANCIAL FORECASTING

Plan	Create	Present
✓ Set the objectives	✓ Gather financial & nonfinancial data	✓ Create a 2-minute summary
✓ Decide on the historical & future periods to present	✓ Discuss where the business is going	✓ Show historical & forecast results side by side
✓ Identify the key drivers (financial and nonfinancial)	✓ Create the forecast	✓ Make the forecast a part of your monthly financial rhythm

Here are the steps in the plan phase:

- Set the objectives.
- Decide on the historical and future periods to present.
- Identify the key drivers (financial and nonfinancial).

Set the Objectives

Step one is to write down the primary goals and objectives of the forecast you're about to create. This is the "begin with the end in mind" step. It helps you define what success will look like once your forecast is complete.

In my consulting work (whether internal or external), I always begin by having a discussion with my client about what they're trying to achieve. I write down the one to three big picture objectives we want to accomplish and get the client's buy-in that I've captured the essence of what we need to accomplish. There's something magical about narrowing the objectives to just one to three and actually writing them down and talking about them upfront.

For example, one company summarized its objectives as follows:

1. Implement a reliable financial forecasting/projections process.
2. Ensure the forecast can be easily updated and published monthly.

The company was growing and wanted to become a more metrics-driven organization. The forecast would help the CEO plan and manage the key drivers/metrics of financial performance at the overall company level. Then she planned to drive that same kind of focus down to the more operational levels of the different divisions of the company.

She was increasing the number of locations and taking on more debt to help finance the growth. She knew the company needed to become more focused on the key drivers of financial performance to ensure the growth was profitable and to help her manage the risk associated with taking on more debt. The forecast was a central part of how she would more closely manage both financial performance and risk on a monthly basis. The forecast would also help her plan and manage their different legal entities at the overall company/consolidated level.

The "easily updated and published monthly" part of the second objective was critical. The CEO had previously been through a forecasting exercise, but the result was too difficult to maintain and, therefore, provided limited benefits for only a couple months.

In another example, I was brought in to help a company that had grown nicely to over $75 million in annual revenues. The majority shareholder had built the business over time but never really put in place an experienced accountant as the controller or CFO. Then a combination of a tough economy, and intense competition, put a big squeeze on cash flow. The squeeze required the company to borrow everything it had available on their existing bank line and they violated a number of critical debt covenants.

The credit line was large (for both the company and the bank). And the owner had personally guaranteed the credit line as well. If the bank pulled the credit line, the company would fail and the owner would have to file personal bankruptcy because the debt would overwhelm his personal net worth. It was a big problem.

The bank was very nervous and was taking a somewhat activist role as a result. The bank was asking lots of questions about financial results and not getting timely answers. They wanted timely financial statements and reliable answers about what results would look like in the coming months so they could evaluate the company (and its credit risk—banks hate losing money).

Here is how we defined the primary objectives:

1. Establish confidence and credibility with the bank.
2. Produce timely and accurate financial statements.
3. Provide a monthly financial forecast for the next twelve months.

The written objectives helped keep everyone focused on what we were there to accomplish.

Decide on the Historical and Future Periods to Present

Consider how many months of historical financial statements to include in your forecast. When possible, two to three years of historical monthly results is ideal because they provide insight into the drivers of results, trends over time, month-to-month variations in results, etc. The numbers will help you assess where the company has been according to the actual results.

Forecast periods should be monthly for the upcoming twelve to eighteen months. Although there are times when you may want to forecast farther into the future (e.g., when presenting a long-term plan, raising capital, or attracting a lender), twelve to eighteen months is sufficient for month-to-month decision making.

It is important to maintain the twelve to eighteen month forecast horizon as each month goes by. For example, let's say you begin the process with eighteen months in your forecast. Once the first month goes by, you now have seventeen months in the forecast. The forecast horizon shrinks each month unless you regularly add months to the end of the forecast horizon. This process of maintaining the number of periods in the forecast is what makes the forecast a "rolling forecast."

A rolling forecast means that when a month is over you add a month to the end of the forecast period. That way you always have a defined period in your forecast.

I am a big fan of the rolling forecast because it helps you get out of the mindset of thinking only in terms of the calendar or fiscal year. It helps you think in terms of a more practical planning horizon rather than the traditional compliance driven reporting periods.

Having said that, it is not always necessary to adhere to the strict definition of a rolling forecast. I generally let three months or so go by before I add to the end of the forecast period. I allow the forecast period to "flex" a little bit from month-to-month unless there are meaningful changes going on in the business that will clearly impact the future periods. I allow some flexibility in defining and updating the forecast horizon. It really depends on what's going on in the business, the nature of the planning cycle, and the types of decisions the forecast informs.

When it comes to how frequently to update the numbers in the forecast period, I encourage you to look at the forecast period as consisting of the "near term" and the "longer term." The near term is the next three to nine months or so. The longer term would be the next twelve to eighteen months.

The near term is where you want to answer the question "What's about to happen?" You want your leadership team and other users of the forecast to have a clear view of what financial results are likely to be in the near future. As a result, pay very close attention to the next three to nine months in the forecast and update those numbers monthly.

The longer term is more about answering the question "What could happen?" This is more of a "What happens if" kind of question. What happens if we expand our operation in the northeast? What happens if a major competitor opens a new store near our flagship location? These numbers would generally be updated only when there is an event or something has happened in the business that makes it necessary to change the forecast. Or there is some planning or discussions going on in the business and you want to forecast a range of options or possibilities. Otherwise, I generally update these numbers in the forecast once a quarter or so.

Identify the Key Drivers (Financial and Nonfinancial)

Identify the key drivers that impact your results (and, therefore, your financial statements). Because the forecast doesn't consist of actual transactions, consider the larger influences that will drive expected results in the financial statements.

A retailer might consider:

- number of customers/transactions,
- customer traffic trends,
- competitive threats,
- average ticket,
- gross profit margin,
- current operating expense structure,
- company growth plans,
- lease expiration dates,
- the impact of seasonality on inventory levels,
- existing debt service requirements, and
- capital expenditure plans.

Next, consider what drives those balances at the highest level possible. Figure 4-2 lists the financial statement categories and suggestions for forecasting those balances that this same retailer might consider.

Figure 4-2

THE APPROACH TO FORECASTING

Financial Statement Categories	Forecast Approach
INCOME STATEMENT	
Revenues	Number of customers/transactions X average revenue per ticket
Gross profit	Gross margin X revenues
Operating expenses	Estimates by expense category based on trend, budget, etc.
BALANCE SHEET	
Cash	The net impact of all other assumptions
Accounts receivable	Days sales outstanding (DSO) X average daily revenues
Inventory	Days inventory outstanding (DIO) X average daily COGS
Property and equipment	Estimate based on growth and maintenance capital expenditure plans
Accounts payable	Days payables outstanding (DPO) X average daily expenses
Third party and related party debt (short-term and long-term)	Estimates based on debt service requirements and borrowing plans
Owner's equity related accounts	Estimates based on investment and owner distribution plans

You will be using these key drivers when you develop your forecast assumptions.

CREATE

In this phase of the forecasting process, you will insert historical financial and nonfinancial information into your forecasting tool. Then, use information about trends and metrics in those results, together with information from management and others, and begin creating the assumptions that will drive the forecast results.

Here are the steps:

- Gather financial and nonfinancial data
- Discuss where the business is going
- Create the forecast

Gather Financial and Nonfinancial Data

Most accounting systems have a feature for exporting financial statements that show each month in the range side-by-side so that information can be easily imported or pasted into your forecasting software or spreadsheet. I generally export an income statement and balance sheet for the historical periods and rely on the forecasting tool to create the statement of cash flows.

Also, gather and incorporate the nonfinancial data. For example, a retailer may have identified the number of customers or transactions and average ticket to be key drivers, because the number of customers/transactions multiplied by the average ticket = sales. You would go to your POS system and gather (or export) the number of customers/transactions for the period identified in the Plan phase.

A construction company might gather the number of open projects and average revenue per project. There is generally a handful or so of nonfinancial data to gather. Keep in mind that you want to be sure you create a repeatable process here because this will need to be exported each month going forward.

Discuss Where the Business Is Going

One of the benefits of the financial forecasting process is that it forces you to think deeply about your company's vision and strategy. For example, what are the three most critical goals or initiatives for the coming year? Is the company planning to grow slowly or aggressively? Are there plans to bid on projects similar to the ones in the past, or is the company moving into new markets or new customer segments?

Answering these types of strategic questions helps you think beyond the day to day work inside the business and encourages conversations with management about their goals, strategies, and expectations.

Create the Forecast

Now it is time to enter the assumptions that will create the forecast results. You will draw on a unique blend of historical results and trends, your understanding of the company's vision and strategy, and your intuition about what is most likely to happen financially.

In the forecasting process, we are going to use some "hacks," or short-cuts, to estimate what we believe the end results of cash flow and financial results will be. Here are my suggestions on the approach to forecasting each of these components of a full set of financial statements.

Revenues. Think for a minute at a very summary level about this question: What two numbers could you multiply together to arrive at revenues?

- For a retailer it might be number of customers × average ticket = revenues.
- For a law firm it might be hours incurred by attorneys × average billing rate = revenues.
- For a wholesaler of fuel it might be gallons of fuel sold × average selling price per gallon = revenues.

You want to do this exercise at the highest (most summary) level possible. Notice how the key drivers almost always include nonfinancial data (like number of customers in the retail example, hours worked in the law firm example, and gallons sold in the fuel wholesaler example).

Gross Margin. In most cases, it is best to use a single gross margin estimate to drive gross profit (and, therefore, cost of goods sold).

Operating and Nonoperating Expenses. I generally prefer to enter operating expenses by line item based on existing trends, budget, expectation, etc.

Days Sales Outstanding (DSO). DSO is the number of days of average sales sitting in accounts receivable (A/R). It is a good shortcut for forecasting A/R on the balance sheet each month. Accounts receivable at the end of a month is a function of the balance at the end of the prior month plus revenues minus collections. Rather than estimating the amount to be collected, using DSO multiplied by average daily revenues is a reliable way to estimate the ending balance. Then the forecast model can calculate how much was assumed to be collected during the month for the statement of cash flows.

Days Inventory Outstanding (DIO). DIO is the number of days of cost of goods sold sitting in inventory. It is a good shortcut for forecasting the inventory on the balance sheet each month. Inventory at the end of a month is a function of the balance at the end of the prior month plus purchases minus cost of goods sold. Rather than estimating the amount of inventory purchased during the month, multiply DIO by average daily cost of goods sold to estimate the ending inventory balance. Then the forecast model can calculate how much was assumed to be purchased during the month.

Capital Expenditures. This amount is used to estimate capital expenditures for each month, which are a function of management plans and expectations for capital expenditures.

Days Payable Outstanding (DPO). DPO is the number of days of expenses sitting in accounts payable (A/P). It is a good shortcut for forecasting A/P on the balance sheet each month. The model can then adjust cash according to the change in payables for the month.

Principal Payments on Debt. This is used to estimate principal payments on debt based on existing debt service requirements as well as any additional long-term plans for borrowing or paying debt down faster than the existing schedule. You need to look at your debt structure and whether you have long-term debt where you are making regular monthly payments and if you have, or also have, short-term debt like a bank line of credit or similar debt.

Other Asset and Liability Accounts. One of the main items to consider here is income taxes. This will depend on the kind of entity your business is in. If you are in an S corp or LLC or other pass-through type entity then one of the main items here is distributions to owners. These are very big assumptions so pay close attention to them.

Owner Distributions. Use a dollar amount to estimate owner distributions.

Now the Fun Part!

Now it's time to sit down and crank through all the assumptions necessary to create a forecast of the income statement, balance sheet, and cash flows for the coming months.

This is a *very* interative process. You will drop in some revenue estimates and then realize that the revenues for the year look way too big…or way too low. Same with your operating expenses. You will look back at the prior month's gross margins and see they have been bouncing around from month to month. So you will go a little deeper to see what's causing those changes. You will try to figure out if they will continue. Then once you begin making assumptions about balance sheet accounts, you may see that the balances each month don't make sense relative to historical balances. You will find yourself thinking about every component of the financial statements as you work through this process.

The key is to use the time you spend making assumptions and looking at the results of the forecast financial statements to deepen your understanding of what drives financial results in your business. Remember, this is a top-down, rather than a bottom-up, exercise. So try not to allow yourself to drive your forecast assumptions down to the lowest level possible. Stay up at the 30,000-foot level.

> "The key assumptions, those that have the greatest effect on forecasted cash flow, highlight where management competency is required and become the KPIs."
>
> —Robert H. Hacker, *Billion Dollar Company*

Once you've drafted your forecast, take some time to review your work. Here are some questions to consider:

- Given my knowledge of the business and existing trends, does the forecast make sense?
- Does it show the company as a net generator of cash or a net user of cash?
- When discussing the forecast results with the CEO, will he or she be surprised by the overall plan for the company's financial future?
- When discussing the critical assumptions and key drivers used to create the forecast with the CEO, will he or she agree that the assumptions and drivers seem reasonable?

In my consulting work, I review the highlights of the forecast with my client to get feedback on whether the big picture view of the forecast creates any surprises or concerns. We walk through the critical assumptions and the key drivers of performance. We look at the existing trends and talk about specific strategies being employed in the business that might alter those trends.

The last step in this phase is to make the necessary changes to the forecast based on the feedback you have received. Armed with input from management and others you can go back and make any changes necessary to create the "final" version of the forecast. There's almost always going to be some tweaking to do. Maybe margins are likely to go up two months from now because the company is rolling out a brand new, high margin product. Or there is a large capital expenditure being planned six months from now that you were not aware of.

Present

Presenting the forecast is more art than science. It's about how you turn the forecast into insight for your leadership team; how you present the key insights will ultimately determine the success of your forecast process.

Here are the steps:

- Create a 2-minute summary
- Show historical and forecast results side-by-side
- Make the forecast part of your Monthly Financial Rhythm

Create a 2-Minute Summary

Creating a reliable forecast and effectively communicating it to your audience starts with making the forecast results simple and easy to understand. I have found that getting laser focused on simplifying the results of the forecast pays big dividends. You want to present the assumptions and results at the highest level possible to start. Then be prepared to drill down and provide the next layer of information after the high level view is fully presented and understood.

Figure 4-3 is an example of a 2-minute summary. There is one key insight because the expansion into Texas is a significant event. It will take about one minute to communicate that summary. The remainder of the meeting with the CEO or the board will be spent answering questions about the key assumptions and the conclusion. The number of questions will be determined by the degree to which your conclusions or insights come as a surprise.

Figure 4-3
THE 2-MINUTE SUMMARY

Based on our growth plan for the coming year, we will need to raise $1.1 million to $1.3 million in cash by June 30. The primary driver of the need to raise cash is the plan for launching a new division in Texas. The expansion is forecast at $3.0 to $3.5 million driven primarily by the capital expenditure and first-year operating losses.

Show Historical and Forecast Results Side-by-Side

There's something almost magical about presenting financial results and financial statements where each month is shown side-by-side. It makes the trends and direction in the business jump off the page at you. And I always like to show actual months for the year next to the forecast months as a way to give the reader a view into actual and projected performance for the year.

After the 2-minute summary, this is one of the first views of the detailed forecast results I provide. It helps clarify the forecast results because you can see the forecast periods together with actual results. It highlights what has been happening in the recent past, educates the reader about the financial statements in general, and helps everyone get comfortable with the assumptions used to create the forecast.

Make the Forecast Part of Your Monthly Financial Rhythm

Life, business, and money all move in a rhythm or cycle. So does financial management and forecasting. The forecast is a key part of your monthly financial rhythm. You don't want all the benefits of having a forecast to be a one-time thing and then get put on a shelf somewhere or forgotten. Include it in your monthly financial reporting package. That way you make it a part of how you plan and manage the financial side of the business each month.

Figure 4-4
THE MONTHLY FINANCIAL RHYTHM

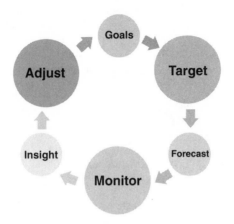

I refer to this natural financial rhythm in business as the TARGET, MONITOR, ADJUST cycle. It's about setting financial goals and TARGETS, MONITORING forecast and actual financial results, and making ADJUSTMENTS in strategy and execution inside the company when results differ from the target or expectation.

Business (and money) moves in a rhythm, a cycle. So does financial management.

It's a monthly rhythm designed to improve decision making and provide financial feedback inside your company. A fast feedback loop makes it possible to quickly identify strategies that need to change because financial results are not in line with expectations.

Target – The targets are the key financial and nonfinancial goals that drive from your vision and strategy. A company in restructuring mode would have different targets than a company trying to scale and grow. The targets can change as well depending on short-term financial goals. For example, one quarter you might have specific goals related to collecting receivables faster. Another quarter might include a focus on reducing certain expense categories. There will generally be three to five targets at any time. But the mix of targets/metrics will vary during the year.

Monitor – Monitoring is about creating financial forecasts (expected financial results) and actual results (historical financials). Forecasts are a fully modeled set of financial statements over at least the next six to eighteen months. Actuals are financial statements and the key drivers of financial performance. The combination of the forecast and actuals results is converted into insight (not just numbers or financial statements).

Adjust – You and your team then use insightful financial information to determine whether the specific action plans and strategies being executed throughout the company are working as expected. Your management team is on board because they understand the financial goals and the related metrics being tracked. You have helped them learn how to use the monthly financial information to compare the actions they are taking in the field to the implications in the financial statements. Now they have a tight link between their plans and the actual financial results. Adjustments to strategies and tactics in the field can be made quickly when the financial information suggests something is not working the way you intended.

The cycle continues every month by making any necessary changes to the financial goals and targets and the resulting forecast/expectations. It's a monthly financial rhythm designed to help you focus on what matters most. It's the key to turning financial information into insight.

> "The more often we forecast, the quicker we will be able to act to correct any problems with our process."
>
> —Steve Morlidge and Steve Player, *Future Ready: How to Master Business Forecasting*

Each month your forecast should be updated as follows:

- Load actual results when the month is over.
- Compare actuals to the forecast.
- Make any necessary changes to the forecast months.
- Add any necessary periods to the end of the forecast.
- Work closely with the leadership team to identify action items that can drive improvements in profitability and cash flow.

That's the recipe for creating a reliable financial forecast. Now let's walk through the plan, create, present process in a step-by-step fashion with a real world example in the next chapter. You will see how the process unfolds and look at the before and after results.

Chapter 5

A Real World Example–ABC Construction Company

"Just because an opportunity doesn't pique my imagination or look too exciting at first, I've learned not to discount it."

—GEORGE FOREMAN, *KNOCKOUT ENTREPRENEUR*

Now I would like to bring the process of creating a reliable financial forecast together for you in an example. This example is a sort of mini-case study to help you see how the principles you have learned so far are applied. I will walk through the plan, create, present process in a step-by-step fashion so you see the inside view of how the process unfolds.

The example follows a general contractor in the construction industry who is creating a financial forecast for the first time. ABC Construction's CEO/owner plans to recruit a number of respected and experienced entrepreneurs, executives, and savvy members of the financial community to join his Board of Directors. He wants to take his company to the next level and believes that having people who have "been there and done that" will be critical to his success in growing the company. A reliable financial forecast is one of the tools the CEO and Board of Directors will use to plan and monitor the pace and progress of ABC's growth strategies. The CEO wants to put the forecasting process in place before he begins recruiting board members.

Current annual revenues are about $25 million and the company wants to double that number over the next three years. My role was to work closely with the CFO to plan and implement the forecasting process. Once we got the process up and running, the CFO would maintain the forecast each month going forward.

Building the Forecast

Like a construction project, the three distinct phases of building a forecast are Plan, Create, and Present.

Because the CFO was a spreadsheet "power user," we decided to create the financial model in Excel. It was designed so it could be updated monthly and would track the existing financial statement format.

Plan

Set the Objectives

The objectives were heavily influenced by the CEO's desire to create a tool to support a robust financial planning and monitoring process for the board. He wanted the forecast to become a part of their monthly financial rhythm and he wanted to avoid creating a labor-intensive process. The objectives were documented as:

1. Implement a reliable financial forecasting/projection process to provide a clear view of likely financial results in order to evaluate various growth plans and strategies.

2. Make the process a "top-down" rather than a "bottom-up" exercise. That way we will require very little input or effort from others in the company.

Figure 5-1
THE RECIPE FOR FINANCIAL FORECASTING

Plan	Create	Present
✓ Set the objectives	✓ Gather financial & nonfinancial data	✓ Create a 2-minute summary
✓ Decide on the historical & future periods to present	✓ Discuss where the business is going	✓ Show historical & forecast results side by side
✓ Identify the key drivers (financial and nonfinancial)	✓ Create the forecast	✓ Make the forecast a part of your monthly financial rhythm

3. Incorporate the forecast into the monthly financial reporting process for the Board.

These three objectives would guide the implementation and would be referred back to at the end of the project to ensure we accomplished the original intent of the forecast. (This is a very important benefit of stating your goals in writing at the very beginning of the process. It helps you get clear on the overall objectives *and* gives you something to look back on after the forecasting process is up and running to ensure you achieved the original goals.)

Decide on the Historical and Future Periods to Present

The most recent financial statements are from June 30 of the current year. Eighteen months of actual financial data and eighteen months of forecast data were included in the financial model to provide a solid view of recent monthly financial performance and extend the forecast through the end of the next calendar year.

Figures 5-2 through 5-7 show the monthly income statements, balance sheets, and statements of cash flows for the prior year and for the six months ended June 30 of the current year.

Figure 5-2: INCOME STATEMENTS – Prior Year

ABC Construction Company	Actual Jan	Actual Feb	Actual Mar	Actual Apr	Actual May	Actual Jun	Actual Jul	Actual Aug	Actual Sep	Actual Oct	Actual Nov	Actual Dec	Actual Year
Number of projects	15	16	14	15	15	17	19	19	15	14	15	15	15
Average revenue per project	$129,550	$133,599	$155,738	$115,181	$132,477	$128,581	$109,294	$130,551	$143,284	$135,096	$119,785	$99,108	$1,602,864
Revenues	$1,943,256	$2,137,582	$2,180,333	$1,727,710	$1,987,156	$2,185,871	$2,076,578	$2,480,467	$2,149,258	$1,891,347	$1,796,780	$1,486,619	$24,042,956
Total	1,943,256	2,137,582	2,180,333	1,727,710	1,987,156	2,185,871	2,076,578	2,480,467	2,149,258	1,891,347	1,796,780	1,486,619	24,042,956
Cost of good sold	1,663,427	1,791,293	1,855,464	1,489,286	1,683,121	1,840,504	1,731,866	2,120,799	1,818,272	1,647,363	1,520,076	1,250,246	20,411,717
Gross profit	279,829	346,288	324,870	238,424	304,035	345,368	344,712	359,668	330,986	243,984	276,704	236,372	3,631,239
	14.4%	16.2%	14.9%	13.8%	15.3%	15.8%	16.6%	14.5%	15.4%	12.9%	15.4%	15.9%	15.1%
OPERATING EXPENSES													
Employee wages & taxes	101,467	104,638	121,978	110,638	127,252	112,612	110,490	111,441	116,897	116,870	103,625	110,690	1,348,598
Rent	14,750	14,820	14,760	15,357	17,663	14,800	14,800	14,800	14,800	14,800	14,800	14,800	180,950
Advertising & marketing	5,328	5,495	6,405	4,737	5,448	5,288	4,495	5,369	5,893	5,556	4,926	4,076	63,016
Insurance	12,480	12,870	15,003	11,096	12,762	12,387	10,529	12,576	13,803	13,014	11,539	9,547	147,606
Telephone & utilities	3,544	3,655	4,260	3,151	3,624	3,517	2,990	3,571	3,920	3,696	3,277	2,711	41,916
Travel, meals & entertainment	2,853	2,942	3,430	2,537	2,917	2,832	2,407	2,875	3,155	2,975	2,638	2,183	33,744
Professional fees	4,500	4,641	5,410	4,001	4,602	4,466	3,796	4,535	4,977	4,693	4,161	3,443	53,223
Office expenses	2,980	3,073	3,582	2,649	3,047	2,958	2,514	3,003	3,296	3,108	2,755	2,280	35,246
Depreciation & amortization	5,475	5,475	5,475	5,475	5,475	5,475	5,475	5,475	5,475	5,475	5,475	10,350	70,575
All other	5,496	5,668	6,607	4,886	5,620	5,455	4,637	5,538	6,079	5,731	5,082	4,205	65,003
Total	158,873	163,276	186,910	164,527	188,411	169,790	162,132	169,184	178,295	175,918	158,278	164,284	2,039,877
Operating income	120,956	183,012	137,960	73,897	115,624	175,578	182,580	190,484	152,691	68,066	118,426	72,088	1,591,362
Interest expense	8,237	8,162	8,087	8,012	7,937	7,862	7,787	7,712	7,637	7,562	7,487	7,412	93,900
Other expense (income)	0	0	0	0	0	0	0	0	0	0	0	0	0
Total	8,237	8,162	8,087	8,012	7,937	7,862	7,787	7,712	7,637	7,562	7,487	7,412	93,900
Pretax income	$112,718	$174,850	$129,872	$65,885	$107,686	$167,716	$174,792	$182,771	$145,054	$60,504	$110,938	$64,676	$1,497,462
As % of revenues	5.8%	8.2%	6.0%	3.8%	5.4%	7.7%	8.4%	7.4%	6.7%	3.2%	6.2%	4.4%	6.2%
EBITDA	126,431	188,487	143,435	79,372	121,099	181,053	188,055	195,959	158,166	73,541	123,901	82,438	1,661,937

Figure 5-3: **BALANCE SHEETS – Prior Year**

ABC Construction Company	Actual Jan	Actual Feb	Actual Mar	Actual Apr	Actual May	Actual Jun	Actual Jul	Actual Aug	Actual Sep	Actual Oct	Actual Nov	Actual Dec
ASSETS												
Cash	$1,143,471	$1,340,165	$1,381,504	$1,024,989	$1,234,820	$1,445,426	$1,515,779	$2,053,095	$1,763,674	$1,470,734	$1,439,566	$826,313
Accounts receivable	2,946,231	2,924,855	2,968,462	2,916,631	2,876,887	2,920,605	2,858,308	2,932,722	2,975,707	3,013,534	2,959,630	2,915,032
Inventory	163,581	181,494	144,385	189,063	222,726	185,916	237,872	174,248	137,882	104,935	150,537	188,045
Costs & estimated earnings in excess of billings on uncompleted contracts	209,134	132,807	162,429	248,684	193,571	236,761	219,316	162,362	142,879	216,396	217,033	245,177
Other current assets	24,876	25,876	25,876	25,876	25,876	25,876	25,876	23,376	23,376	23,376	23,376	23,376
Total current assets	4,487,293	4,605,197	4,682,656	4,405,243	4,553,880	4,814,584	4,857,149	5,345,802	5,043,518	4,828,975	4,790,142	4,197,942
Machinery & equipment	202,333	202,333	217,878	217,878	221,468	221,468	221,468	245,457	245,457	249,927	249,927	249,927
Furniture, fixtures & equipment	251,590	251,590	251,590	251,590	251,590	251,590	251,590	251,590	251,590	251,590	251,590	251,590
Gross property	453,923	453,923	469,468	469,468	473,058	473,058	473,058	497,047	497,047	501,517	501,517	501,517
Less: accumulated depreciation	(150,000)	(155,475)	(160,950)	(166,425)	(171,900)	(177,375)	(182,850)	(188,325)	(193,800)	(199,275)	(204,750)	(215,100)
Net property	303,923	298,448	308,518	303,043	301,158	295,683	290,208	308,722	303,247	302,242	296,767	286,417
Total Assets	$4,791,216	$4,903,645	$4,991,174	$4,708,287	$4,855,038	$5,110,267	$5,147,358	$5,654,524	$5,346,765	$5,131,217	$5,086,910	$4,484,359
LIABILITIES & EQUITY												
Accounts payable & accrued liabilities	$1,684,389	$1,813,867	$1,878,845	$1,508,053	$1,704,331	$1,863,697	$1,753,690	$2,147,525	$1,841,185	$1,668,123	$1,539,231	$1,266,001
Short-term notes payable	478,250	468,250	458,250	448,250	438,250	428,250	418,250	408,250	398,250	388,250	378,250	368,250
Billings in excess of costs & estimated earnings on uncompleted contracts	679,321	577,423	560,100	672,120	604,908	623,055	685,361	705,922	649,448	636,459	700,105	721,108
Total current liabilities	2,841,960	2,859,539	2,897,196	2,628,424	2,747,489	2,915,002	2,857,301	3,261,697	2,888,883	2,692,832	2,617,586	2,355,360
Notes payable	1,169,245	1,164,245	1,159,245	1,154,245	1,149,245	1,144,245	1,139,245	1,134,245	1,129,245	1,124,245	1,119,245	1,114,245
Owner's investment	500,000	500,000	500,000	500,000	500,000	500,000	500,000	500,000	500,000	500,000	500,000	500,000
Owner distributions	(570,000)	(645,000)	(720,000)	(795,000)	(870,000)	(945,000)	(1,020,000)	(1,095,000)	(1,170,000)	(1,245,000)	(1,320,000)	(1,720,000)
Retained earnings	850,011	1,024,861	1,154,733	1,220,618	1,328,304	1,496,020	1,670,812	1,853,583	1,998,637	2,059,140	2,170,079	2,234,755
Total equity	780,011	879,861	934,733	925,618	958,304	1,051,020	1,150,812	1,258,583	1,328,637	1,314,140	1,350,079	1,014,755
Total liabilities & equity	$4,791,216	$4,903,645	$4,991,174	$4,708,287	$4,855,038	$5,110,267	$5,147,358	$5,654,524	$5,346,765	$5,131,217	$5,086,910	$4,484,359

Figure 5-4: **STATEMENTS OF CASH FLOWS** – Prior Year

ABC Construction Company	Actual Jan	Actual Feb	Actual Mar	Actual Apr	Actual May	Actual Jun	Actual Jul	Actual Aug	Actual Sep	Actual Oct	Actual Nov	Actual Dec	Actual Year
Pre-tax income	$112,718	$174,850	$129,872	$65,885	$107,686	$167,716	$174,792	$182,771	$145,054	$60,504	$110,938	$64,676	$1,497,462
Depreciation and amortization	5,475	5,475	5,475	5,475	5,475	5,475	5,475	5,475	5,475	5,475	5,475	10,350	70,575
Decrease (increase) in accounts receivable	(15,679)	21,376	(43,607)	51,831	39,743	(43,717)	62,297	(74,414)	(42,985)	(37,827)	53,903	44,599	15,520
Decrease (increase) in inventory	3,425	(17,913)	37,109	(44,679)	(33,662)	36,810	(51,956)	63,624	36,365	32,947	(45,602)	(37,507)	(21,039)
Decrease (increase) in costs & estimated earnings in excess of billings on uncompleted contracts	(11,745)	76,327	(29,622)	(86,255)	55,114	(43,190)	17,446	56,953	19,483	(73,518)	(636)	(28,144)	(47,788)
Decrease (increase) in other current assets	1,250	(1,000)	0	0	0	0	0	2,500	0	0	0	0	2,750
(Decrease) increase in accounts payable & accrued liabilities	(18,902)	129,478	64,979	(370,792)	196,278	159,366	(110,007)	393,835	(306,339)	(173,063)	(128,892)	(273,230)	(437,290)
(Decrease) increase in short-term notes payable	(10,000)	(10,000)	(10,000)	(10,000)	(10,000)	(10,000)	(10,000)	(10,000)	(10,000)	(10,000)	(10,000)	(10,000)	(120,000)
(Decrease) increase in billings in excess of costs & estimated earnings on uncompleted contracts	35,024	(101,898)	(17,323)	112,020	(67,212)	18,147	62,306	20,561	(56,474)	(12,989)	63,646	21,003	76,812
Net cash provided by operating activities	101,566	276,694	136,884	(276,515)	293,421	290,606	150,353	641,305	(209,421)	(208,470)	48,832	(208,254)	1,037,003
CASH FLOWS - INVESTING ACTIVITIES													
Purchase of property and equipment	(23,540)	0	(15,545)	0	(3,590)	0	0	(23,989)	0	(4,470)	0	0	(71,134)
Net cash provided (used) by investing activities	(23,540)	0	(15,545)	0	(3,590)	0	0	(23,989)	0	(4,470)	0	0	(71,134)
CASH FLOWS - FINANCING ACTIVITIES													
Payments on long-term debt	(5,000)	(5,000)	(5,000)	(5,000)	(5,000)	(5,000)	(5,000)	(5,000)	(5,000)	(5,000)	(5,000)	(5,000)	(60,000)
Distributions to owners	(175,000)	(75,000)	(75,000)	(75,000)	(75,000)	(75,000)	(75,000)	(75,000)	(75,000)	(75,000)	(75,000)	(400,000)	(1,325,000)
Net cash provided (used) by financiang activities	(180,000)	(80,000)	(80,000)	(80,000)	(80,000)	(80,000)	(80,000)	(80,000)	(80,000)	(80,000)	(80,000)	(405,000)	(1,385,000)
Increase (decrease) in cash	(101,974)	196,694	41,339	(356,515)	209,831	210,606	70,353	537,316	(289,421)	(292,940)	(31,168)	(613,254)	(419,131)
Cash at beginning of month	1,245,444	1,143,471	1,340,165	1,381,504	1,024,989	1,234,820	1,445,426	1,515,779	2,053,095	1,763,674	1,470,734	1,439,566	1,245,444
Cash at end of month	$1,143,471	$1,340,165	$1,381,504	$1,024,989	$1,234,820	$1,445,426	$1,515,779	$2,053,095	$1,763,674	$1,470,734	$1,439,566	$826,313	$826,313

Figure 5-5: **INCOME STATEMENTS – Current Year**

ABC Construction Company	Actual Jan	Actual Feb	Actual Mar	Actual Apr	Actual May	Actual Jun
Number of projects	15	13	16	18	17	15
Average revenue per project	$142,592	$196,529	$138,358	$108,227	$108,864	$102,081
Revenues	$2,138,875	$2,554,881	$2,213,736	$1,948,087	$1,850,683	$1,531,217
Total	$2,138,875	$2,554,881	$2,213,736	$1,948,087	$1,850,683	1,531,217
Cost of good sold	1,837,294	2,143,545	1,861,752	1,698,732	1,567,529	1,303,066
Gross profit	301,581	411,336	351,984	249,355	283,155	228,151
	14.1%	16.1%	15.9%	12.8%	15.3%	14.9%
OPERATING EXPENSES						
Employee wages & taxes	107,555	106,731	119,538	117,276	134,887	119,369
Rent	15,635	15,116	14,465	16,278	18,723	15,688
Advertising & marketing	5,648	5,604	6,277	5,021	5,775	5,605
Insurance	13,229	13,127	14,703	11,761	13,420	13,130
Telephone & utilities	3,757	3,728	4,175	3,340	3,370	3,729
Travel, meals & entertainment	3,024	3,001	3,361	2,689	3,092	3,002
Professional fees	4,770	4,733	5,301	4,241	4,689	4,734
Office expenses	3,159	3,135	3,511	2,808	3,230	3,135
Depreciation & amortization	5,850	5,850	5,850	5,850	5,850	5,850
All other	5,826	5,781	6,475	5,180	5,957	5,782
Total	168,452	166,807	183,656	174,445	198,995	180,024
Operating income	133,130	244,529	168,328	74,910	84,160	48,128
Interest expense	7,337	7,262	7,187	7,112	7,037	6,962
Other expense (income)	0	0	0	0	0	0
Total	7,337	7,262	7,187	7,112	7,037	6,962
Pretax income	$125,792	$237,267	$161,140	$67,798	$77,122	$41,165
As % of revenues	5.9%	9.3%	7.3%	3.5%	4.2%	2.7%
EBITDA	$138,980	$250,379	$174,178	$80,760	$90,010	$53,978

Figure 5-6: **BALANCE SHEETS – Current Year**

ABC Construction Company	Actual Jan	Actual Feb	Actual Mar	Actual Apr	Actual May	Actual Jun
ASSETS						
Cash	$975,032	$1,323,412	$1,523,480	$1,335,275	$1,176,083	$1,051,409
Accounts receivable	2,850,865	2,927,512	2,971,787	3,010,748	2,955,228	2,709,291
Inventory	243,164	178,857	141,622	107,648	154,674	193,766
Costs & estimated earnings in excess of billings on uncompleted contracts	207,968	318,636	336,610	255,487	250,378	223,443
Other current assets	23,376	23,376	23,376	23,376	23,376	23,376
Total current assets	4,300,404	4,771,793	4,996,875	4,732,535	4,559,738	4,201,284
Machinery & equipment	261,177	261,177	279,929	279,929	279,929	279,929
Furniture, fixtures & equipment	251,590	251,590	251,590	251,590	251,590	251,590
Gross property	512,767	512,767	531,519	531,519	531,519	531,519
Less: accumulated depreciation	(220,950)	(226,800)	(232,650)	(238,500)	(244,350)	(250,200)
Net property	291,817	285,967	298,869	293,019	287,169	281,319
Total Assets	$4,592,221	$5,057,760	$5,295,744	$5,025,554	$4,846,907	$4,482,603
LIABILITIES & EQUITY						
Accounts payable & accrued liabilities	$1,341,438	$1,610,436	$1,777,769	$1,622,104	$1,496,818	$1,244,285
Short-term notes payable	358,250	348,250	338,250	328,250	318,250	308,250
Billings in excess of costs & estimated earnings on uncompleted contracts	742,741	817,016	841,526	774,204	758,720	720,784
Total current liabilities	2,442,430	2,775,702	2,957,545	2,724,557	2,573,788	2,273,319
Notes payable	1,109,245	1,104,245	1,099,245	1,094,245	1,089,245	1,084,245
Owner's investment	500,000	500,000	500,000	500,000	500,000	500,000
Owner distributions	(1,820,000)	(1,920,000)	(2,020,000)	(2,120,000)	(2,220,000)	(2,320,000)
Retained earnings	2,360,547	2,597,813	2,758,954	2,826,751	2,903,874	2,945,039
Total equity	1,040,547	1,177,813	1,238,954	1,206,751	1,183,874	1,125,039
Total liabilities & equity	$4,592,221	$5,057,760	$5,295,744	$5,025,554	$4,846,907	$4,482,603

Figure 5-7: **STATEMENTS OF CASH FLOWS – Current Year**

ABC Construction Company	Actual Jan	Actual Feb	Actual Mar	Actual Apr	Actual May	Actual Jun
Pre-tax income	$125,792	$237,267	$161,140	$67,798	$77,122	$41,165
Depreciation and amortization	5,850	5,850	5,850	5,850	5,850	5,850
Decrease (increase) in accounts receivable	64,166	(76,646)	(44,275)	(38,962)	55,520	245,937
Decrease (increase) in inventory	(55,119)	64,306	37,235	33,975	(47,026)	(39,092)
Decrease (increase) in costs & estimated earnings in excess of billings on uncompleted contracts	37,209	(110,668)	(17,974)	81,123	5,110	26,935
Decrease (increase) in other current assets	0	0	0	0	0	0
(Decrease) increase in accounts payable & accrued liabilities	75,437	268,998	167,333	(155,666)	(125,285)	(252,533)
(Decrease) increase in short-term notes payable	(10,000)	(10,000)	(10,000)	(10,000)	(10,000)	(10,000)
(Decrease) increase in billings in excess of costs & estimated earnings on uncompleted contracts	21,633	74,274	24,510	(67,323)	(15,484)	(37,936)
Net cash provided by operating activities	264,969	453,380	323,820	(83,205)	(54,192)	(19,674)
CASH FLOWS - INVESTING ACTIVITIES						
Purchase of property and equipment	(11,250)	0	(18,752)	0	0	0
Net cash provided (used) by investing activities	(11,250)	0	(18,752)	0	0	0
CASH FLOWS - FINANCING ACTIVITIES						
Payments on long-term debt	(5,000)	(5,000)	(5,000)	(5,000)	(5,000)	(5,000)
Distributions to owners	(100,000)	(100,000)	(100,000)	(100,000)	(100,000)	(100,000)
Net cash provided (used) by financing activities	(105,000)	(105,000)	(105,000)	(105,000)	(105,000)	(105,000)
Increase (decrease) in cash	148,719	348,380	200,068	(188,205)	(159,192)	(124,674)
Cash at beginning of month	826,313	975,032	1,323,412	1,523,480	1,335,275	1,176,083
Cash at end of month	$975,032	$1,323,412	$1,523,480	$1,335,275	$1,176,083	$1,051,409

Because cash is the real bottom line in business, and I am a big fan of simplification when it comes to understanding cash flow, I also created a summary view of cash flow for the same periods as shown in Figures 5-8 and 5-9.

One of the first things you will notice as you look at the financial statements is there are *lots of numbers*. Even a financial person could easily get bogged down in looking through eighteen months of financial statements. The secret at this stage in the process is to keep your review simple and focused on the big picture. Here is how I do it.

Before I look at any historical financial statements, I have an initial discussion with my client about the business and get their big picture view of recent financial performance. That way I get a good sense of what management believes is happening financially before I review their financial statements. This is a great way to get an initial read on whether management is on top of what's going on financially. It also helps me avoid the tendency to drill down with questions about their financials when I am having that initial big picture discussion about the business.

Figure 5-8: **SUMMARY CASH FLOWS** – Prior Year

ABC Construction Company	Actual Jan	Actual Feb	Actual Mar	Actual Apr	Actual May	Actual Jun	Actual Jul	Actual Aug	Actual Sep	Actual Oct	Actual Nov	Actual Dec	Actual Year
Beginning cash balance	$1,245,444	$1,143,471	$1,340,165	$1,381,504	$1,024,989	$1,234,820	$1,445,426	$1,515,779	$2,053,095	$1,763,674	$1,470,734	$1,439,566	$1,245,444
Pre-tax income	112,718	174,850	129,872	65,885	107,686	167,716	174,792	182,771	145,054	60,504	110,938	64,676	1,497,462
Accounts receivable	(15,679)	21,376	(43,607)	51,831	39,743	(43,717)	62,297	(74,414)	(42,985)	(37,827)	53,903	44,599	15,520
Accounts payable	(18,902)	129,478	64,979	(370,792)	196,278	159,366	(110,007)	393,835	(306,339)	(173,063)	(128,892)	(273,230)	(437,290)
Distributions to owners	(175,000)	(75,000)	(75,000)	(75,000)	(75,000)	(75,000)	(75,000)	(75,000)	(75,000)	(75,000)	(75,000)	(400,000)	(1,325,000)
Debt	(15,000)	(15,000)	(15,000)	(15,000)	(15,000)	(15,000)	(15,000)	(15,000)	(15,000)	(15,000)	(15,000)	(15,000)	(180,000)
All other changes, net	9,890	(39,009)	(19,906)	(13,438)	(43,876)	17,242	33,270	125,124	4,849	(52,553)	22,881	(34,297)	10,176
Net cash flow	(101,973)	196,694	41,338	(356,515)	209,831	210,606	70,353	537,316	(289,422)	(292,939)	(31,169)	(613,253)	(419,131)
Ending cash balance	$1,143,471	$1,340,165	$1,381,504	$1,024,989	$1,234,820	$1,445,426	$1,515,779	$2,053,095	$1,763,674	$1,470,734	$1,439,566	$826,313	$826,313

Figure 5-9: **SUMMARY CASH FLOWS – Current Year**

ABC Construction Company	Actual Jan	Actual Feb	Actual Mar	Actual Apr	Actual May	Actual Jun
Beginning cash balance	$826,313	$975,032	$1,323,412	$1,523,480	$1,335,275	$1,176,083
Pre-tax income	125,792	237,267	161,140	67,798	77,122	41,165
Accounts receivable	64,166	(76,646)	(44,275)	(38,962)	55,520	245,937
Accounts payable	75,437	268,998	167,333	(155,666)	(125,285)	(252,533)
Distributions to owners	(100,000)	(100,000)	(100,000)	(100,000)	(100,000)	(100,000)
Debt	(15,000)	(15,000)	(15,000)	(15,000)	(15,000)	(15,000)
All other changes, net	(1,676)	33,762	30,869	53,625	(51,549)	(44,243)
Net cash flow	148,719	348,380	200,068	(188,205)	(159,191)	(124,674)
Ending cash balance	$975,032	$1,323,412	$1,523,480	$1,335,275	$1,176,083	$1,051,409

Once I have the monthly financial statements, the first question I want to answer is: "What's going on with the cash?" This is my starting point for understanding a company's financial statements. I do this by looking at the three largest changes (or drivers) in cash for the most recent periods. Figures 5-8 and 5-9 are summary views of ABC's cash flow that make it easy to see quickly the three largest drivers of cash. Last year, the three largest drivers were pre-tax income of $1.5 million, distributions to owners of $1.3 million, and a reduction in accounts payable of $0.4 million.

That little bit of information tells me the company was profitable last year and they distributed almost 90% of their pre-tax profits to the owners. Very little cash was used to reinvest in the company or pay down debt. That is not necessarily a good or a bad thing. It just provides a quick look at the 30,000-foot view of the drivers of cash. A quick look at the six months of the current year showed pretty much the same picture.

The next step is to look at the income statements to see how the $1.5 million pre-tax profit last year compares to revenues and gross profit. Pre-tax profit is about 6% of the $24 million in sales last year. In many companies, a 6% pre-tax profit margin would be cause for concern. But this isn't necessarily a problem in a company like ABC where gross profit margins are very thin. Pre-tax profit is just over 40% of gross profit.

I also like to look at monthly revenues and pre-tax profits to see how much they vary from month to month. In this case, there are some small swings but nothing big enough to raise red flags or dig into more at this point. And the results for the current year appear to be in line with last year.

Now I take a quick look at the balance sheets. I look at the size of the balance sheet and some of the larger balances that make it up. At December of last year, total assets were $4.5 million and equity was $1.0 million. Those numbers help put a little more context around the $1.5 million of pre-tax profit. Pre-tax profit last year was over 30% of total assets and 150% of equity. Those are healthy percentages (at least on the surface). Then I take a quick look at the accounts receivable, inventory, accounts payable, and debt balances to get a sense for the larger amounts on the balance sheet. None of those balances raise concerns.

Take a few minutes now to walk through the simplified, big picture review process I just outlined as you look at Figures 5-2 through 5-9.

Figure 5-10 shows the work in progress (WIP) schedule at June 30 of the current year. In a construction company, especially one using the percentage completion method of accounting, this is a critically important schedule.

Identify the Key Drivers (Financial and Nonfinancial)

Figures 5-11 and 5-12 show the format for the assumptions sheet where most of the forecast assumptions will be entered. The assumptions sheet brings the relevant information and metrics together in one place. It will be used to review actual results for each driver or metric *and* to enter assumptions for the forecast periods. The shaded rows are the primary drivers that will be used to forecast. Operating expenses are not shown here because those estimates will be entered directly into the income statement.

Figure 5-10: **CONTRACTS IN PROGRESS – Current Year**

CONTRACT	TOTAL CONTRACT		FROM INCEPTION TO JUNE 30						AT JUNE 30	
ABC Construction Company	Revenues	Estimated Gross Profit	Total Costs Incurred	Percent Complete	Revenue Earned	Gross Profit	Billed to Date	Estimated Costs to Complete	Costs & Estimated Earnings in Excess of Billings	Billings in Excess of Costs & Estimated Earnings
Project 1	$1,554,605	$233,191	$145,356	11%	$171,007	$25,651	$224,500	$1,176,059		$53,493
Project 2	745,690	149,138	387,759	65%	484,699	96,940	409,800	208,793	74,899	
Project 3	460,000	59,800	112,056	28%	128,800	16,744	164,000	288,144		35,200
Project 4	800,000	88,000	534,000	75%	600,000	66,000	695,000	178,000		95,000
Project 5	925,000	166,500	189,625	25%	231,250	41,625	185,000	568,875	46,250	
Project 6	1,202,500	204,425	39,923	4%	48,100	8,177	-	958,152	48,100	
Project 7	962,000	153,920	775,757	96%	923,520	147,763	1,005,000	32,323		81,480
Project 8	769,600	92,352	541,798	80%	615,680	73,882	725,000	135,450		109,320
Project 9	615,680	104,666	178,855	35%	215,488	36,633	246,800	332,159		31,312
Project 10	700,000	91,000	401,940	66%	462,000	60,060	500,000	207,060		38,000
Project 11	320,000	52,800	120,240	45%	144,000	23,760	184,675	146,960		40,675
Project 12	256,000	44,800	63,360	30%	76,800	13,440	133,873	147,840		57,073
Project 13	750,000	105,000	96,750	15%	112,500	15,750	58,306	548,250	54,194	
Project 14	600,000	66,000	357,780	67%	402,000	44,220	500,486	176,220		98,486
Project 15	480,000	86,400	236,160	60%	288,000	51,840	368,745	157,440		80,745
	$11,141,075	$1,697,991	$4,181,359		$4,903,843	$722,484	$5,401,185	$5,261,725	$223,443	$720,784

Figure 5-11: FORECAST ASSUMPTIONS SUMMARY – Prior Year

ABC Construction Company	Actual Jan	Actual Feb	Actual Mar	Actual Apr	Actual May	Actual Jun	Actual Jul	Actual Aug	Actual Sep	Actual Oct	Actual Nov	Actual Dec
Change in number of projects	2	1	(2)	1	0	2	2	0	(4)	(1)	1	0
Number of projects	15	16	14	15	15	17	19	19	15	14	15	15
Change in average revenue per project from same month prior year	NA	NA	NA	NA	NA	NA	NA	NA	NA	NA	NA	NA
Average revenue per project	$129,550	$133,599	$155,738	$115,181	$132,477	$128,581	$109,294	$130,551	$143,284	$135,096	$119,785	$99,108
Sales	$1,943,256	$2,137,582	$2,180,333	$1,727,710	$1,987,156	$2,185,871	$2,076,578	$2,480,467	$2,149,258	$1,891,347	$1,796,780	$1,486,619
Gross margin	14.4%	16.2%	14.9%	13.8%	15.3%	15.8%	16.6%	14.5%	15.4%	12.9%	15.4%	15.9%
Days Sales Outstanding (DSO)	NA	NA	43.6	40.5	44.2	47.2	41.1	41.3	39.2	39.1	43.9	47.4
Average daily sales (last two months)	NA	NA	$68,014	$71,965	$65,134	$61,914	$69,550	$71,041	$75,951	$77,162	$67,343	$61,469
Accounts receivable	$2,946,231	$2,924,855	$2,968,462	$2,916,631	$2,876,887	$2,920,605	$2,858,308	$2,932,722	$2,975,707	$3,013,534	$2,959,630	$2,915,032
Days Inventory Outstanding (DIO)	NA	NA	2.5	3.1	4.0	3.5	4.1	2.9	2.1	1.6	2.6	3.6
Average daily cost of sales (last two months)	NA	NA	$57,579	$60,779	$55,746	$52,873	$58,727	$59,539	$64,211	$65,651	$57,761	$52,791
Inventory	$163,581	$181,494	$144,385	$189,064	$222,726	$185,916	$237,872	$174,248	$137,883	$104,935	$150,538	$188,045
Capital expenditures	0	0	(15,545)	0	(3,590)	0	0	(23,989)	0	(4,470)	0	0
Days Payable Outstanding (DPO)	NA	NA	31.6	24.0	29.5	34.0	28.9	35.0	27.9	24.7	25.8	23.2
Average daily cost of sales & expenses	NA	NA	$59,513	$62,839	$57,726	$54,791	$60,689	$61,353	$66,034	$67,637	$59,768	$54,686
Accounts payable	$1,684,389	$1,813,867	$1,878,845	$1,508,053	$1,704,331	$1,863,697	$1,753,690	$2,147,525	$1,841,185	$1,668,123	$1,539,231	$1,266,001
Principal payments on short-term debt	(10,000)	(10,000)	(10,000)	(10,000)	(10,000)	(10,000)	(10,000)	(10,000)	(10,000)	(10,000)	(10,000)	(10,000)
Principal payments on long-term debt	(5,000)	(5,000)	(5,000)	(5,000)	(5,000)	(5,000)	(5,000)	(5,000)	(5,000)	(5,000)	(5,000)	(5,000)
Owner distributions	$(75,000)	$(75,000)	$(75,000)	$(75,000)	$(75,000)	$(75,000)	$(75,000)	$(75,000)	$(75,000)	$(75,000)	$(75,000)	$(400,000)
Billings in excess liability as % of trailing 2 months of revenue	NA	NA	13.7%	15.6%	15.5%	16.8%	16.4%	16.6%	14.3%	13.7%	17.3%	19.6%
Trailing 2 months of revenue	NA	NA	4,080,838	4,317,915	3,908,043	3,714,866	4,173,027	4,262,449	4,557,045	4,629,725	4,040,605	3,688,127
Billings in excess liability	679,321	577,423	560,100	672,120	604,908	623,055	685,361	705,922	649,448	636,459	700,105	721,108
Relationship of costs and estimated earnings asset to the liability	30.8%	23.0%	29.0%	37.0%	32.0%	38.0%	32.0%	23.0%	22.0%	34.0%	31.0%	34.0%
Costs and estimated earnings asset	209,134	132,807	162,429	248,684	193,571	236,761	219,316	162,362	142,879	216,396	217,033	245,177

Figure 5-12: **FORECAST ASSUMPTIONS SUMMARY – Current Year**

ABC Construction Company	Actual Jan	Actual Feb	Actual Mar	Actual Apr	Actual May	Actual Jun
Change in number of projects	0	(2)	3	2	(1)	(2)
Number of projects	15	13	16	18	17	15
Change in average revenue per project from same month prior year	10.1%	47.1%	-11.2%	-6.0%	-17.8%	-20.6%
Average revenue per project	$142,592	$196,529	$138,358	$108,227	$108,864	$102,081
Sales	$2,138,875	$2,554,881	$2,213,736	$1,948,087	$1,850,683	$1,531,217
Gross margin	14.1%	16.1%	15.9%	12.8%	15.3%	14.9%
Days Sales Outstanding (DSO)	52.1	37.4	37.4	43.4	46.7	48.1
Average daily sales (last two months)	$54,723	$78,229	$79,477	$69,364	$63,313	$56,365
Accounts receivable	$2,850,865	$2,927,512	$2,971,787	$3,010,748	$2,955,228	$2,709,291
Days Inventory Outstanding (DIO)	5.3	2.7	2.1	1.8	2.8	4.1
Average daily cost of sales (last two months)	$46,172	$66,347	$66,755	$59,341	$54,438	$47,843
Inventory	$243,164	$178,857	$141,622	$107,648	$154,674	$193,766
Capital expenditures	$(11,250)	$-	$(18,752)	$-	$-	$-
Days Payable Outstanding (DPO)	28.0	23.6	25.8	26.4	26.5	24.9
Average daily cost of sales & expenses	$47,976	$68,364	$68,825	$61,363	$56,459	$49,923
Accounts payable	$1,341,438	$1,610,436	$1,777,769	$1,622,104	$1,496,818	$1,244,285
Principal payments on short-term debt	(10,000)	(10,000)	(10,000)	(10,000)	(10,000)	(10,000)
Principal payments on long-term debt	(5,000)	(5,000)	(5,000)	(5,000)	(5,000)	(5,000)
Owner distributions	$(100,000)	$(100,000)	$(100,000)	$(100,000)	$(100,000)	$(100,000)
Billings in excess liability as % of trailing 2 months of revenue	22.6%	17.4%	17.6%	18.6%	20.0%	21.3%
Trailing 2 months of revenue	3,283,398	4,693,756	4,768,617	4,161,823	3,798,770	3,381,900
Billings in excess liability	742,741	817,016	841,526	774,204	758,720	720,784
Relationship of costs and estimated earnings asset to the liability	28.0%	39.0%	40.0%	33.0%	33.0%	31.0%
Costs and estimated earnings asset	207,968	318,636	336,610	255,487	250,378	223,443

CREATE

Gather Financial and Nonfinancial Data

ABC's accounting system made it easy to export eighteen months of income statements and balance sheets, with each month shown side-by-side. The statement of cash flows was created in the Excel financial model to generate that statement for both the historical and forecast periods. The number of open projects per month came from ABC's project management system and prior month WIP schedules, which were manually entered for each of the eighteen months of actual data.

Discuss Where the Business Is Going

ABC's CFO was very involved in the business, had a good handle on the market, and knew what kinds of projects were in progress. Most of our discussions about the future were with the CEO. We talked about the general trend in gross margins for new projects and his existing plans for bidding on projects outside of their specialty area (with much larger customers than ABC had worked with in the past).

Create the Forecast

The first thing we did before making any forecast assumptions was to sit down and review the historical financial statements and the key drivers. This is where we want to review what has been driving results in the recent past, look for trends and key insights, and be on the lookout for any surprises that need to be considered in the forecast.

Then we combined (1) our insights from our review of key drivers over the last eighteen months, (2) information we gathered from our discussion with the CEO, and (3) our knowledge and intuition about the business, and sat down to begin the work of making forecast assumptions in the forecast model. Because this was a new process for ABC, the first few iterations of the forecast focused on the next six months. Once we were comfortable with the results and insights, we then forecast the following year by month.

Let's look at each of the key drivers in the forecast assumptions sheet and how we went about entering assumptions for the next six months.

Change in Number of Projects. The key assumption was that ABC would add one to two net new projects each month. We used an estimate of two for July and one for each of the months of August through December. For ABC, the fourth quarter is traditionally slow; in the prior year, the number of open projects was flat for the fourth quarter. But in the upcoming fourth quarter, ABC expected to win some bids from larger customers for projects outside of the company's usual focus.

Change in Average Revenue Per Project from the Same Month Prior Year. The average monthly revenue per project fluctuated in the actuals. The trend was toward increasing average revenue. For the next six months, we estimated a 3% increase in average revenue per project for each month.

Gross Margin. Overall gross margins did not vary widely in the actuals. The estimate was 15% for July through September and 14% for October through December. The lower gross margin for the fourth quarter factored in the new projects outside of its normal project type that ABC expected to win.

Operating and Nonoperating Expenses. Operating expenses were not included in the assumptions sheet because those estimates were entered directly into the income statement section of the forecast model. The estimates were based on a combination of actual results, budget, and current expectations.

Days Sales Outstanding. A company's DSO (the number of days of average sales sitting in accounts receivable) will fluctuate based on the number and size of open projects and whether a specific customer is slow to pay its invoices. Over the past eighteen months, ABC's DSO ranged from the high 30s to the low 50s. An estimate of 43 was used for the months of July through September, and was increased for the months of October through December. The higher DSO estimate in the fourth quarter is related to ABC's expectation that the new, larger company projects will pay slower than its typical customers. (This assumption has a big impact on the forecast results.)

Days Inventory Outstanding. DIO is the number of days of cost of goods sold sitting in inventory. ABC did not carry much inventory and was working on several initiatives to reduce inventory further.

The estimate of days of inventory on hand for each of the next six months was 3.0.

Capital Expenditures. A dollar amount was used to estimate capital expenditures for each month based on the company's plans for upgrading certain equipment and their existing growth and reinvestment plans.

Days Payable Outstanding. ABC's DPO (the number of days of expenses sitting in accounts payable) did not vary much from month to month and was expected to continue at recent levels. The estimate for the next six months was 25.0.

Principal Payments on Debt. ABC was paying a flat amount each month to reduce principal on debt, and those amounts were used as the estimates. The management team had discussed plans to pay debt down more aggressively but these plans were not included in the assumptions. (More to come on that assumption in the Present phase.)

Owner Distributions. It was assumed that owner distributions would stop in August. (This assumption will also be discussed in the Present phase.)

Billings in Excess Liability as a Percent of Trailing Two Months of Revenues. Because we are not rolling up numbers from a work in progress schedule, a top-down approach is needed to estimate the balance in the percentage completion related balance sheet accounts; using a percent of trailing revenues is a reliable approach. This percentage had bounced around from month to month. Based on recent actuals and expectations, 18% was estimated for each of the next six months.

Relationship of Costs and Estimated Earnings Asset to the Related Liability. Over the last eighteen months, the relationship of costs

Figure 5-13: **FORECAST ASSUMPTIONS SUMMARY – Next Six Months**

ABC Construction Company	Forecast Jul	Forecast Aug	Forecast Sep	Forecast Oct	Forecast Nov	Forecast Dec
Change in number of projects	2	1	1	1	1	1
Number of projects	17	18	19	20	21	22
Change in average revenue per project from same month prior year	3.0%	3.0%	3.0%	3.0%	3.0%	3.0%
Average revenue per project	$112,572	$134,467	$147,582	$139,149	$123,379	$102,081
Sales	$1,913,730	$2,420,414	$2,804,065	$2,782,982	$2,590,956	$2,245,785
Gross margin	15.0%	15.0%	15.0%	14.0%	14.0%	14.0%
Days Sales Outstanding (DSO)	43.0	43.0	43.0	50.0	50.0	55.0
Average daily sales (last two months)	$57,416	$72,236	$87,075	$93,117	$89,566	$80,612
Accounts receivable	$2,468,879	$3,106,136	$3,744,210	$4,655,873	$4,478,282	$4,433,680
Days Inventory Outstanding (DIO)	3.0	3.0	3.0	3.0	3.0	3.0
Average daily cost of sales (last two months)	$48,829	$61,400	$74,013	$79,614	$77,026	$69,327
Inventory	$146,487	$184,201	$222,040	$238,841	$231,079	$207,980
Capital expenditures	$(25,000)	$-	$-	$(15,000)	$-	$-
Days Payable Outstanding (DPO)	25.0	25.0	25.0	25.0	25.0	25.0
Average daily cost of sales & expenses	$50,880	$63,485	$76,107	$81,716	$79,137	$71,446
Accounts payable	$1,271,998	$1,587,121	$1,902,665	$2,042,889	$1,978,429	$1,786,157
Principal payments on short-term debt	(10,000)	(10,000)	(10,000)	(10,000)	(10,000)	(10,000)
Principal payments on long-term debt	(5,000)	(5,000)	(5,000)	(5,000)	(5,000)	(5,000)
Owner distributions	$(100,000)	$-	$-	$-	$-	$-
Billings in excess liability as % of trailing 2 months of revenue	18.0%	18.0%	18.0%	18.0%	18.0%	18.0%
Trailing 2 months of revenue	3,444,947	4,334,144	5,224,479	5,587,047	5,373,938	4,836,741
Billings in excess liability	620,091	780,146	940,406	1,005,668	967,309	870,613
Relationship of costs and estimated earnings asset to the liability	32.0%	32.0%	32.0%	32.0%	32.0%	32.0%
Costs and estimated earnings asset	198,429	249,647	300,930	321,814	309,539	278,596

and estimated earnings to the related liability account (expressed as a percentage) varied from a low of 22% to a high of 40%; over the past six months, the trend was in the mid 30s. We decided to use 32% as the estimate for the next six months.

Figures 5-13 and 5-14 show the key assumptions for each of the next six months of the current year and for each month of the next year.

Figures 5-15 through 5-20 show the forecast for the monthly income statements, balance sheets, and statements of cash flows for the next six months (including actual results for the first six months of the current year) and for the next year. Remember, the forecasting

Figure 5-14: **FORECAST ASSUMPTIONS SUMMARY – Next Year**

ABC Construction Company	Forecast Jan	Forecast Feb	Forecast Mar	Forecast Apr	Forecast May	Forecast Jun	Forecast Jul	Forecast Aug	Forecast Sep	Forecast Oct	Forecast Nov	Forecast Dec
Change in number of projects	0	(2)	(2)	0	1	2	1	1	(2)	(1)	0	(1)
Number of projects	22	20	18	18	19	21	22	23	21	20	20	19
Change in average revenue per project from same month prior year	3.0%	3.0%	3.0%	3.0%	3.0%	3.0%	3.0%	3.0%	3.0%	3.0%	3.0%	3.0%
Average revenue per project	$146,869	$202,425	$142,509	$111,474	$112,130	$105,144	$115,950	$138,501	$152,010	$143,324	$127,080	$105,144
Sales	$3,231,127	$4,048,504	$2,565,166	$2,006,530	$2,130,463	$2,208,015	$2,550,890	$3,185,533	$3,192,207	$2,866,471	$2,541,605	$1,997,728
Gross margin	14.0%	14.0%	15.0%	15.0%	15.0%	15.0%	15.0%	15.0%	15.0%	15.0%	15.0%	15.0%
Days Sales Outstanding (DSO)	50.0	50.0	45.0	44.0	43.0	43.0	43.0	43.0	43.0	43.0	43.0	43.0
Average daily sales (last two months)	$91,282	$121,327	$110,228	$76,195	$68,950	$72,308	$79,315	$95,607	$106,296	$100,978	$90,135	$75,656
Accounts receivable	$4,564,094	$6,066,359	$4,960,252	$3,352,577	$2,964,845	$3,109,243	$3,410,549	$4,111,103	$4,570,714	$4,342,053	$3,875,788	$3,253,188
Days Inventory Outstanding (DIO)	3.0	3.0	3.0	3.0	3.0	3.0	3.0	3.0	3.0	3.0	3.0	3.0
Average daily cost of sales (last two months)	$46,313	$104,341	$94,368	$64,766	$58,607	$61,462	$67,418	$81,266	$90,351	$85,831	$76,614	$64,307
Inventory	$138,938	$313,024	$283,105	$194,297	$175,822	$184,385	$202,253	$243,798	$271,054	$257,494	$229,843	$192,922
Capital expenditures	(15,000)	0	(10,000)	0	0	(25,000)	0	0	(50,000)	0	0	0
Days Payable Outstanding (DPO)	25.0	25.0	25.0	25.0	25.0	25.0	25.0	25.0	25.0	25.0	25.0	25.0
Average daily cost of sales & expenses	$47,399	$106,510	$96,592	$66,939	$60,726	$63,632	$69,591	$83,451	$92,546	$88,035	$78,827	$66,529
Accounts payable	$1,184,979	$2,662,757	$2,414,810	$1,673,466	$1,518,161	$1,590,800	$1,739,773	$2,086,283	$2,313,639	$2,200,863	$1,970,669	$1,663,219
Principal payments on short-term debt	(10,000)	(10,000)	(10,000)	(10,000)	(10,000)	(10,000)	(31,375)	(31,375)	(31,375)	(31,375)	(31,375)	(31,375)
Principal payments on long-term debt	(5,000)	(5,000)	(5,000)	(5,000)	(5,000)	(5,000)	(170,708)	(170,708)	(170,708)	(170,708)	(170,708)	(170,708)
Owner distributions	$-	$-	$(100,000)	$(100,000)	$(100,000)	$(100,000)	$(100,000)	$(100,000)	$(100,000)	$(100,000)	$(100,000)	$(600,000)
Billings in excess liability as % of trailing 2 months of revenue	18.0%	18.0%	18.0%	18.0%	18.0%	18.0%	18.0%	18.0%	18.0%	18.0%	18.0%	18.0%
Trailing 2 months of revenue	5,476,912	7,279,631	6,613,670	4,571,696	4,136,993	4,338,478	4,758,905	5,736,423	6,377,740	6,058,678	5,408,076	4,539,333
Billings in excess liability	985,844	1,310,334	1,190,461	822,905	744,659	780,926	856,603	1,032,556	1,147,993	1,090,562	973,454	817,080
Relationship of costs and estimated earnings asset to the liability	32.0%	32.0%	32.0%	32.0%	32.0%	32.0%	32.0%	32.0%	32.0%	32.0%	32.0%	32.0%
Costs and estimated earnings asset	315,470	419,307	380,947	263,330	238,291	249,896	274,113	330,418	367,358	348,980	311,505	261,466

Figure 5-15: INCOME STATEMENTS – Current Year with Forecast

ABC Construction Company	Actual Jan	Actual Feb	Actual Mar	Actual Apr	Actual May	Actual Jun	Forecast Jul	Forecast Aug	Forecast Sep	Forecast Oct	Forecast Nov	Forecast Dec	Forecast Current Year
Number of projects	15	13	16	18	17	15	17	18	19	20	21	22	22
Average revenue per project	$142,592	$196,529	$138,358	$108,227	$108,864	$102,081	$112,572	$134,467	$147,582	$139,149	$123,379	$102,081	$1,227,064
Revenues	$2,138,875	$2,554,881	$2,213,736	$1,948,087	$1,850,683	$1,531,217	$1,913,730	$2,420,414	$2,804,065	$2,782,982	$2,590,956	$2,245,785	$26,995,412
Total	2,138,875	2,554,881	2,213,736	1,948,087	1,850,683	1,531,217	1,913,730	2,420,414	2,804,065	2,782,982	2,590,956	2,245,785	26,995,412
Cost of good sold	1,837,294	2,143,545	1,861,752	1,698,732	1,567,529	1,303,066	1,626,671	2,057,352	2,383,455	2,393,365	2,228,222	1,931,375	23,032,357
Gross profit	301,581	411,336	351,984	249,355	283,155	228,151	287,060	363,062	420,610	389,617	362,734	314,410	3,963,055
	14.1%	16.1%	15.9%	12.8%	15.3%	14.9%	15.0%	15.0%	15.0%	14.0%	14.0%	14.0%	14.7%
OPERATING EXPENSES													
Employee wages & taxes	107,555	106,731	119,538	117,276	134,887	119,369	120,562	121,768	122,986	124,216	125,458	126,712	1,447,058
Rent	15,635	15,116	14,465	16,278	18,723	15,888	16,500	16,500	16,500	16,500	16,500	16,500	194,906
Advertising & marketing	5,648	5,604	6,277	5,021	5,775	5,605	5,661	5,718	5,775	5,833	5,891	5,950	68,760
Insurance	13,229	13,127	14,703	11,761	13,420	13,130	13,261	13,394	13,528	13,663	13,800	13,938	160,952
Telephone & utilities	3,757	3,728	4,175	3,340	3,370	3,729	3,766	3,803	3,841	3,880	3,919	3,958	45,265
Travel, meals & entertainment	3,024	3,001	3,361	2,689	3,092	3,002	3,200	3,200	3,200	3,200	3,200	3,200	37,369
Professional fees	4,770	4,733	5,301	4,241	4,689	4,734	5,000	5,000	5,000	5,000	5,000	5,000	58,469
Office expenses	3,159	3,135	3,511	2,808	3,230	3,135	3,167	3,198	3,230	3,262	3,295	3,328	38,458
Depreciation & amortization	5,850	5,850	5,850	5,850	5,850	5,850	5,850	5,850	5,850	5,850	5,850	5,850	70,200
All other	5,826	5,781	6,475	5,180	5,957	5,782	6,000	6,000	6,000	6,000	6,000	6,000	71,001
Total	168,452	166,807	183,656	174,445	198,995	180,024	182,967	184,431	185,910	187,404	188,912	190,436	2,192,439
Operating income	133,130	244,529	168,328	74,910	84,160	48,128	104,092	178,631	234,700	202,214	173,821	123,974	1,770,616
Interest expense	7,337	7,262	7,187	7,112	7,037	6,962	6,887	6,812	6,737	6,662	6,587	6,512	83,100
Other expense (income)	0	0	0	0	0	0	0	0	0	0	0	0	0
Total	7,337	7,262	7,187	7,112	7,037	6,962	6,887	6,812	6,737	6,662	6,587	6,512	83,100
Pretax income	$125,792	$237,267	$161,140	$67,798	$77,122	$41,165	$97,205	$171,818	$227,962	$195,551	$167,234	$117,461	$1,687,516
As % of revenues	5.9%	9.3%	7.3%	3.5%	4.2%	2.7%	5.1%	7.1%	8.1%	7.0%	6.5%	5.2%	6.3%
EBITDA	$138,980	$250,379	$174,178	$80,760	$90,010	$53,978	109,942	184,481	240,550	208,064	179,671	129,824	1,840,816

Figure 5-16: BALANCE SHEETS – Current Year with Forecast

ABC Construction Company	Actual Jan	Actual Feb	Actual Mar	Actual Apr	Actual May	Actual Jun	Forecast Jul	Forecast Aug	Forecast Sep	Forecast Oct	Forecast Nov	Forecast Dec
ASSETS												
Cash	$975,032	$1,323,412	$1,523,480	$1,335,275	$1,176,083	$1,051,409	$1,254,188	$1,165,845	$1,133,265	$560,805	$813,697	$731,685
Accounts receivable	2,850,865	2,927,512	2,971,787	3,010,748	2,955,228	2,709,291	2,468,879	3,106,136	3,744,210	4,655,873	4,478,282	4,433,680
Inventory	243,164	178,857	141,622	107,648	154,674	193,766	146,487	184,201	222,040	238,840	231,079	207,980
Costs & estimated earnings in excess of billings on uncompleted contracts	207,968	318,636	336,610	255,487	250,378	223,443	198,429	249,647	300,930	321,814	309,539	278,596
Other current assets	23,376	23,376	23,376	23,376	23,376	23,376	23,376	23,376	23,376	23,376	23,376	23,376
Total current assets	4,300,404	4,771,793	4,996,875	4,732,535	4,559,738	4,201,284	4,091,359	4,729,205	5,423,821	5,800,708	5,855,973	5,675,317
Machinery & equipment	261,177	261,177	279,929	279,929	279,929	279,929	304,929	304,929	304,929	319,929	319,929	319,929
Furniture, fixtures & equipment	251,590	251,590	251,590	251,590	251,590	251,590	251,590	251,590	251,590	251,590	251,590	251,590
Gross property	512,767	512,767	531,519	531,519	531,519	531,519	556,519	556,519	556,519	571,519	571,519	571,519
Less: accumulated depreciation	(220,950)	(226,800)	(232,650)	(238,500)	(244,350)	(250,200)	(256,050)	(261,900)	(267,750)	(273,600)	(279,450)	(285,300)
Net property	291,817	285,967	298,869	293,019	287,169	281,319	300,469	294,619	288,769	297,919	292,069	286,219
Total Assets	$4,592,221	$5,057,760	$5,295,744	$5,025,554	$4,846,907	$4,482,603	$4,391,828	$5,023,824	$5,712,590	$6,098,627	$6,148,042	$5,961,536
LIABILITIES & EQUITY												
Accounts payable & accrued liabilities	$1,341,438	$1,610,436	$1,777,769	$1,622,104	$1,496,818	$1,244,285	$1,271,998	$1,587,121	$1,902,665	$2,042,889	$1,978,429	$1,786,157
Short-term notes payable	358,250	348,250	338,250	328,250	318,250	308,250	298,250	288,250	278,250	268,250	258,250	248,250
Billings in excess of costs & estimated earnings on uncompleted contracts	742,741	817,016	841,526	774,204	758,720	720,784	620,091	780,146	940,406	1,005,668	967,309	870,613
Total current liabilities	2,442,430	2,775,702	2,957,545	2,724,557	2,573,788	2,273,319	2,190,339	2,655,517	3,121,321	3,316,807	3,203,988	2,905,020
Notes payable	1,109,245	1,104,245	1,099,245	1,094,245	1,089,245	1,084,245	1,079,245	1,074,245	1,069,245	1,064,245	1,059,245	1,054,245
Owner's investment	500,000	500,000	500,000	500,000	500,000	500,000	500,000	500,000	500,000	500,000	500,000	500,000
Owner distributions	(1,820,000)	(1,920,000)	(2,020,000)	(2,120,000)	(2,220,000)	(2,320,000)	(2,420,000)	(2,420,000)	(2,420,000)	(2,420,000)	(2,420,000)	(2,420,000)
Retained earnings	2,360,547	2,597,813	2,758,954	2,826,751	2,903,874	2,945,039	3,042,244	3,214,062	3,442,024	3,637,575	3,804,809	3,922,271
Total equity	1,040,547	1,177,813	1,238,954	1,206,751	1,183,874	1,125,039	1,122,244	1,294,062	1,522,024	1,717,575	1,884,809	2,002,271
Total liabilities & equity	$4,592,221	$5,057,760	$5,295,744	$5,025,554	$4,846,907	$4,482,603	$4,391,828	$5,023,824	$5,712,590	$6,098,627	$6,148,042	$5,961,536

Figure 5-17: STATEMENTS OF CASH FLOWS – Current Year with Forecast

ABC Construction Company	Actual Jan	Actual Feb	Actual Mar	Actual Apr	Actual May	Actual Jun	Forecast Jul	Forecast Aug	Forecast Sep	Forecast Oct	Forecast Nov	Forecast Dec	Forecast Current Year
Pre-tax income	$125,792	$237,267	$161,140	$67,798	$77,122	$41,165	$97,205	$171,818	$227,962	$195,551	$167,234	$117,461	$1,687,516
Depreciation and amortization	5,850	5,850	5,850	5,850	5,850	5,850	5,850	5,850	5,850	5,850	5,850	5,850	70,200
Decrease (increase) in accounts receivable	64,166	(76,646)	(44,275)	(38,962)	55,520	245,937	240,412	(637,257)	(638,073)	(911,663)	177,591	44,602	(1,518,648)
Decrease (increase) in inventory	(55,119)	64,306	37,235	33,975	(47,026)	(39,092)	47,279	(37,714)	(37,839)	(16,801)	7,762	23,099	(19,935)
Decrease (increase) in costs & estimated earnings in excess of billings on uncompleted contracts	37,209	(110,668)	(17,974)	81,123	5,110	26,935	25,014	(51,218)	(51,283)	(20,884)	12,275	30,943	(33,420)
Decrease (increase) in other current assets	0	0	0	0	0	0	0	0	0	0	0	0	0
(Decrease) increase in accounts payable & accrued liabilities	75,437	268,998	167,333	(155,666)	(125,285)	(252,533)	27,713	315,123	315,543	140,224	(64,460)	(192,272)	520,155
(Decrease) increase in short-term notes payable	(10,000)	(10,000)	(10,000)	(10,000)	(10,000)	(10,000)	(10,000)	(10,000)	(10,000)	(10,000)	(10,000)	(10,000)	(120,000)
(Decrease) increase in billings in excess of costs & estimated earnings on uncompleted contracts	21,633	74,274	24,510	(67,323)	(15,484)	(37,936)	(100,693)	160,055	160,261	65,262	(38,360)	(96,695)	149,505
Net cash provided by operating activities	264,969	453,380	323,820	(83,205)	(54,192)	(19,674)	332,779	(83,343)	(27,580)	(552,460)	257,892	(77,012)	735,374
CASH FLOWS - INVESTING ACTIVITIES													
Purchase of property and equipment	(11,250)	0	(18,752)	0	0	0	(25,000)	0	0	(15,000)	0	0	(70,002)
Net cash provided (used) by investing activities	(11,250)	0	(18,752)	0	0	0	(25,000)	0	0	(15,000)	0	0	(70,002)
CASH FLOWS - FINANCING ACTIVITIES													
Payments on long-term debt	(5,000)	(5,000)	(5,000)	(5,000)	(5,000)	(5,000)	(5,000)	(5,000)	(5,000)	(5,000)	(5,000)	(5,000)	(60,000)
Distributions to owners	(100,000)	(100,000)	(100,000)	(100,000)	(100,000)	(100,000)	(100,000)	0	0	0	0	0	(700,000)
Net cash provided (used) by financing activities	(105,000)	(105,000)	(105,000)	(105,000)	(105,000)	(105,000)	(105,000)	(5,000)	(5,000)	(5,000)	(5,000)	(5,000)	(760,000)
Increase (decrease) in cash	148,719	348,380	200,068	(188,205)	(159,192)	(124,674)	202,779	(88,343)	(32,580)	(572,460)	252,892	(82,012)	(94,628)
Cash at beginning of month	826,313	975,032	1,323,412	1,523,480	1,335,275	1,176,083	1,051,409	1,254,188	1,165,845	1,133,265	560,805	813,697	826,313
Cash at end of month	$975,032	$1,323,412	$1,523,480	$1,335,275	$1,176,083	$1,051,409	$1,254,188	$1,165,845	$1,133,265	$560,805	$813,697	$731,685	$731,685

108

Figure 5-18: INCOME STATEMENTS – Next Year

ABC Construction Company	Forecast Jan	Forecast Feb	Forecast Mar	Forecast Apr	Forecast May	Forecast Jun	Forecast Jul	Forecast Aug	Forecast Sep	Forecast Oct	Forecast Nov	Forecast Dec	Forecast Next Year
Number of projects	22	20	17	19	18	16	18	19	20	21	22	23	23
Average revenue per project	$146,869	$202,425	$142,509	$111,474	$112,130	$105,144	$115,950	$138,501	$152,010	$143,324	$127,080	$105,144	$1,407,976
Revenues	$3,231,127	$4,048,504	$2,565,166	$2,006,530	$2,130,463	$2,208,015	$2,550,890	$3,185,533	$3,192,207	$2,866,471	$2,541,605	$1,997,728	$32,524,239
Total	3,231,127	4,048,504	2,565,166	2,006,530	2,130,463	2,208,015	2,550,890	3,185,533	3,192,207	2,866,471	2,541,605	1,997,728	32,524,239
Cost of good sold	2,778,769	3,481,713	2,180,391	1,705,551	1,810,893	1,876,813	2,168,256	2,707,703	2,713,376	2,436,501	2,160,364	1,698,069	27,718,400
Gross profit	452,358	566,791	384,775	300,980	319,569	331,202	382,633	477,830	478,831	429,971	381,241	299,659	4,805,840
	14.0%	14.0%	15.0%	15.0%	15.0%	15.0%	15.0%	15.0%	15.0%	15.0%	15.0%	15.0%	14.8%
OPERATING EXPENSES													
Employee wages & taxes	128,000	128,000	128,000	128,000	128,000	128,000	128,000	128,000	128,000	128,000	128,000	128,000	1,536,000
Rent	16,500	16,500	16,500	16,500	16,500	16,500	16,500	16,500	16,500	16,500	16,500	16,500	198,000
Advertising & marketing	5,817	5,773	6,465	5,172	5,949	5,774	5,831	5,890	5,949	6,008	6,068	6,129	70,823
Insurance	13,626	13,521	15,144	12,114	13,823	13,524	13,659	13,795	13,933	14,073	14,214	14,356	165,781
Telephone & utilities	3,869	3,840	4,300	3,440	3,471	3,840	3,879	3,918	3,957	3,996	4,036	4,077	46,623
Travel, meals & entertainment	3,115	3,091	3,462	2,769	3,185	3,092	3,296	3,296	3,296	3,296	3,296	3,296	38,490
Professional fees	6,000	6,000	6,000	6,000	6,000	6,000	6,000	6,000	6,000	6,000	6,000	6,000	72,000
Office expenses	3,254	3,229	3,616	2,893	3,327	3,229	3,262	3,294	3,327	3,360	3,394	3,428	39,612
Depreciation & amortization	6,000	6,000	6,000	6,000	6,000	6,000	6,000	6,000	6,000	6,000	6,000	6,000	72,000
All other	7,000	7,000	7,000	7,000	7,000	7,000	7,000	7,000	7,000	7,000	7,000	7,000	84,000
Total	193,181	192,953	196,487	189,888	193,255	192,958	193,426	193,693	193,962	194,233	194,508	194,785	2,323,330
Operating income	259,177	373,837	188,287	111,091	126,315	138,244	189,207	284,137	284,869	235,737	186,733	104,874	2,482,510
Interest expense	6,437	6,362	6,287	6,212	6,137	6,062	5,052	4,042	3,031	2,021	1,010	0	52,656
Other expense (income)													
Total	6,437	6,362	6,287	6,212	6,137	6,062	5,052	4,042	3,031	2,021	1,010	0	52,656
Pretax income	$252,740	$367,475	$182,000	$104,879	$120,177	$132,181	$184,155	$280,096	$281,838	$233,716	$185,722	$104,874	$2,429,854
As % of revenues	7.8%	9.1%	7.1%	5.2%	5.6%	6.0%	7.2%	8.8%	8.8%	8.2%	7.3%	5.2%	7.5%
EBITDA	265,177	379,837	194,287	117,091	132,315	144,244	195,207	290,137	290,869	241,737	192,733	110,874	2,554,510

109

Figure 5-19: **BALANCE SHEETS – Next Year**

ABC Construction Company	Forecast Jan	Forecast Feb	Forecast Mar	Forecast Apr	Forecast May	Forecast Jun	Forecast Jul	Forecast Aug	Forecast Sep	Forecast Oct	Forecast Nov	Forecast Dec
ASSETS												
Cash	$376,232	$756,786	$1,626,352	$2,327,431	$2,536,304	$2,478,825	$2,248,156	$1,956,228	$1,710,971	$1,738,997	$1,812,724	$1,367,253
Accounts receivable	4,564,094	6,066,359	4,960,252	3,352,577	2,964,845	3,109,243	3,410,549	4,111,103	4,570,714	4,342,053	3,875,788	3,253,188
Inventory	138,938	313,024	283,105	194,297	175,822	184,385	202,253	243,797	271,054	257,494	229,843	192,922
Costs & estimated earnings in excess of billings on uncompleted contracts	315,470	419,307	380,947	263,330	238,291	249,896	274,113	330,418	367,358	348,980	311,505	261,466
Other current assets	23,376	23,376	23,376	23,376	23,376	23,376	23,376	23,376	23,376	23,376	23,376	23,376
Total current assets	5,418,110	7,578,852	7,274,033	6,161,011	5,938,637	6,045,725	6,158,447	6,664,923	6,943,472	6,710,899	6,253,237	5,098,205
Machinery & equipment	334,929	334,929	344,929	344,929	344,929	369,929	369,929	369,929	419,929	419,929	419,929	419,929
Furniture, fixtures & equipment	251,590	251,590	251,590	251,590	251,590	251,590	251,590	251,590	251,590	251,590	251,590	251,590
Gross property	586,519	586,519	596,519	596,519	596,519	621,519	621,519	621,519	671,519	671,519	671,519	671,519
Less: accumulated depreciation	(291,300)	(297,300)	(303,300)	(309,300)	(315,300)	(321,300)	(327,300)	(333,300)	(339,300)	(345,300)	(351,300)	(357,300)
Net property	295,219	289,219	293,219	287,219	281,219	300,219	294,219	288,219	332,219	326,219	320,219	314,219
Total Assets	$5,713,329	$7,868,071	$7,567,252	$6,448,230	$6,219,856	$6,345,944	$6,452,666	$6,953,142	$7,275,691	$7,037,118	$6,573,456	$5,412,424
LIABILITIES & EQUITY												
Accounts payable & accrued liabilities	$1,184,979	$2,662,757	$2,414,810	$1,673,466	$1,518,161	$1,590,800	$1,739,773	$2,086,283	$2,313,639	$2,200,863	$1,970,669	$1,663,219
Short-term notes payable	238,250	228,250	218,250	208,250	198,250	188,250	156,875	125,500	94,125	62,750	31,375	0
Billings in excess of costs & estimated earnings on uncompleted contracts	985,844	1,310,334	1,190,461	822,905	744,659	780,926	856,603	1,032,556	1,147,993	1,090,562	973,454	817,080
Total current liabilities	2,409,073	4,201,340	3,823,521	2,704,621	2,461,070	2,559,976	2,753,251	3,244,339	3,555,757	3,354,175	2,975,498	2,480,299
Notes payable	1,049,245	1,044,245	1,039,245	1,034,245	1,029,245	1,024,245	853,538	682,830	512,123	341,415	170,708	0
Owner's investment	500,000	500,000	500,000	500,000	500,000	500,000	500,000	500,000	500,000	500,000	500,000	500,000
Owner distributions	(2,420,000)	(2,420,000)	(2,520,000)	(2,620,000)	(2,720,000)	(2,820,000)	(2,920,000)	(3,020,000)	(3,120,000)	(3,220,000)	(3,320,000)	(3,920,000)
Retained earnings	4,175,011	4,542,486	4,724,486	4,829,364	4,949,542	5,081,723	5,265,878	5,545,973	5,827,811	6,061,528	6,247,250	6,352,125
Total equity	2,255,011	2,622,486	2,704,486	2,709,364	2,729,542	2,761,723	2,845,878	3,025,973	3,207,811	3,341,528	3,427,250	2,932,125
Total liabilities & equity	$5,713,329	$7,868,071	$7,567,252	$6,448,230	$6,219,856	$6,345,944	$6,452,666	$6,953,142	$7,275,691	$7,037,118	$6,573,456	$5,412,424

Figure 5-20: **STATEMENTS OF CASH FLOWS – Next Year**

ABC Construction Company	Forecast Jan	Forecast Feb	Forecast Mar	Forecast Apr	Forecast May	Forecast Jun	Forecast Jul	Forecast Aug	Forecast Sep	Forecast Oct	Forecast Nov	Forecast Dec	Forecast Current Year
Pre-tax income	$252,740	$367,475	$182,000	$104,879	$120,177	$132,181	$184,155	$280,096	$281,838	$233,716	$185,722	$104,874	$2,429,854
Depreciation and amortization	6,000	6,000	6,000	6,000	6,000	6,000	6,000	6,000	6,000	6,000	6,000	6,000	72,000
Decrease (increase) in accounts receivable	(130,414)	(1,502,265)	1,106,107	1,607,675	387,732	(144,398)	(301,306)	(700,555)	(459,610)	228,661	466,265	622,599	1,180,491
Decrease (increase) in inventory	69,041	(174,086)	29,919	88,808	18,475	(8,563)	(17,868)	(41,545)	(27,256)	13,560	27,651	36,922	15,058
Decrease (increase) in costs & estimated earnings in excess of billings on uncompleted contracts	(36,874)	(103,837)	38,359	117,618	25,039	(11,606)	(24,217)	(56,305)	(36,940)	18,378	37,475	50,040	17,131
Decrease (increase) in other current assets	0	0	0	0	0	0	0	0	0	0	0	0	0
(Decrease) increase in accounts payable & accrued liabilities	(601,177)	1,477,778	(247,946)	(741,345)	(155,305)	72,638	148,973	346,510	227,356	(112,776)	(230,194)	(307,450)	(122,938)
(Decrease) increase in short-term notes payable	(10,000)	(10,000)	(10,000)	(10,000)	(10,000)	(10,000)	(31,375)	(31,375)	(31,375)	(31,375)	(31,375)	(31,375)	(248,250)
(Decrease) increase in billings in excess of costs & estimated earnings on uncompleted contracts	115,231	324,489	(119,873)	(367,555)	(78,247)	36,267	75,677	175,953	115,437	(57,431)	(117,109)	(156,374)	(53,534)
Net cash provided by operating activities	(335,453)	385,554	984,566	806,080	313,872	72,521	40,039	(21,220)	75,450	298,734	344,435	325,236	3,289,813
CASH FLOWS - INVESTING ACTIVITIES													
Purchase of property and equipment	(15,000)	0	(10,000)	0	0	(25,000)	0	0	(50,000)	0	0	0	(100,000)
Net cash provided (used) by investing activities	(15,000)	0	(10,000)	0	0	(25,000)	0	0	(50,000)	0	0	0	(100,000)
CASH FLOWS - FINANCING ACTIVITIES													
Payments on long-term debt	(5,000)	(5,000)	(5,000)	(5,000)	(5,000)	(5,000)	(170,708)	(170,708)	(170,708)	(170,708)	(170,708)	(170,708)	(1,054,245)
Distributions to owners	0	0	(100,000)	(100,000)	(100,000)	(100,000)	(100,000)	(100,000)	(100,000)	(100,000)	(100,000)	(600,000)	(1,500,000)
Net cash provided (used) by financing activities	(5,000)	(5,000)	(105,000)	(105,000)	(105,000)	(105,000)	(270,708)	(270,708)	(270,708)	(270,708)	(270,708)	(770,708)	(2,554,245)
Increase (decrease) in cash	(355,453)	380,554	869,566	701,080	208,872	(57,479)	(230,669)	(291,928)	(245,258)	28,026	73,727	(445,472)	635,568
Cash at beginning of month	731,685	376,232	756,786	1,626,352	2,327,431	2,536,304	2,478,825	2,248,156	1,956,228	1,710,971	1,738,997	1,812,724	731,685
Cash at end of month	$376,232	$756,786	$1,626,352	$2,327,431	$2,536,304	$2,478,825	$2,248,156	$1,956,228	$1,710,971	$1,738,997	$1,812,724	$1,367,253	$1,367,253

process is highly iterative. There were lots of back and forth and tweaks and changes along the way.

PRESENT

Create a 2-Minute Summary

Now we have eighteen months of forecast results *and* eighteen months of actual results for the income statement, balance sheet, and cash flows. That's a lot of financial information. It would be overwhelming to most people. If we just plopped all that detail on the CEO or the board they would probably shut down and put it aside. Or they would get lost in the detail and miss the key insights.

We avoid that problem by providing them with a 2-minute summary of the forecast. We distill the insights and implications of the forecast down to what matters most. In a 2-minute summary we identify and communicate the most important implications and high-level drivers and assumptions. We make the forecast results simple and easy to understand and serve it up on a silver platter.

Figure 5-21 is a summary of the key insights and the primary drivers/assumptions in the forecast created for the CEO.

Figure 5-21
THE 2-MINUTE SUMMARY

We have completed the financial forecast that covers the next 18 months of results. Taxable income is expected to be $1.5 to $1.7 million in the current year and $2.2 to $2.5 million for next year. While profitability is generally aligned with our strategic plan going into the year, there are two important insights that we need to discuss. Each one is influenced by our plans to win projects with a number of new, and very large, customers over the next six months.

In addition to the 2-minute summary, we provided the following:

We have adjusted the distributions to owners from $100,000 per month down to zero beginning in August. We restart the owner *distributions in the forecast in March and assume a larger distribution in December of next year.*

We assume that the previous plan to begin aggressively paying down debt is put on hold until July of next year. The assumption is we will pay debt down to zero by December of next year.

The negative assumptions about owner distributions and debt are driven by the temporary cash shortfall created by the new customers. The new customers are large and we have not done business with them in the past. Our experience with large customers has been that they take longer to pay than our traditional customers. And the problem is usually more pronounced in the early months of a project. As a result, we have increased the DSO assumption and assumed that we will be paid slower than normal between October and April.

Figure 5-22: **SUMMARY CASH FLOWS – Next Six Months**

ABC Construction Company	Forecast Jul	Forecast Aug	Forecast Sep	Forecast Oct	Forecast Nov	Forecast Dec	Forecast Current Year
Beginning cash balance	$1,051,409	$1,254,188	$1,165,845	$1,133,265	$560,805	$813,697	$826,313
Pre-tax income	97,205	171,818	227,962	195,551	167,234	117,461	1,687,516
Accounts receivable	240,412	(637,257)	(638,073)	(911,663)	177,591	44,602	(1,518,648)
Accounts payable	27,713	315,123	315,543	140,224	(64,460)	(192,272)	520,155
Distributions to owners	(100,000)	0	0	0	0	0	(700,000)
Debt	(15,000)	(15,000)	(15,000)	(15,000)	(15,000)	(15,000)	(180,000)
All other changes, net	(47,551)	76,974	76,988	18,428	(12,474)	(36,803)	96,348
Net cash flow	202,778	(88,342)	(32,580)	(572,460)	252,891	(82,012)	(94,628)
Ending cash balance	$1,254,188	$1,165,845	$1,133,265	$560,805	$813,697	$731,685	$731,685

To prepare for the follow-up questions from the CEO, a summary of cash flow was created to highlight the monthly impact on cash. Figures 5-22 and 5-23 are the Summary Cash Flows for the next six months and for the next year. It shows that the primary driver of

Figure 5-23: SUMMARY CASH FLOWS – Next Year

ABC Construction Company	Forecast Jan	Forecast Feb	Forecast Mar	Forecast Apr	Forecast May	Forecast Jun	Forecast Jul	Forecast Aug	Forecast Sep	Forecast Oct	Forecast Nov	Forecast Dec	Forecast Next Year
Beginning cash balance	$731,685	$376,232	$756,786	$1,626,352	$2,327,431	$2,536,304	$2,478,825	$2,248,156	$1,956,228	$1,710,971	$1,738,997	$1,812,724	$731,685
Pre-tax income	252,740	367,475	182,000	104,879	120,177	132,181	184,155	280,096	281,838	233,716	185,722	104,874	2,429,854
Accounts receivable	(130,414)	(1,502,265)	1,106,107	1,607,675	387,732	(144,398)	(301,306)	(700,555)	(459,610)	228,661	466,265	622,599	1,180,491
Accounts payable	(601,177)	1,477,778	(247,946)	(741,345)	(155,305)	72,638	148,973	346,510	227,356	(112,776)	(230,194)	(307,450)	(122,938)
Distributions to owners	0	0	(100,000)	(100,000)	(100,000)	(100,000)	(100,000)	(100,000)	(100,000)	(100,000)	(100,000)	(600,000)	(1,500,000)
Debt	(15,000)	(15,000)	(15,000)	(15,000)	(15,000)	(15,000)	(202,083)	(202,083)	(202,083)	(202,083)	(202,083)	(202,083)	(1,302,495)
All other changes, net	138,399	52,567	(55,595)	(155,130)	(28,732)	(2,901)	39,592	84,103	7,242	(19,493)	(45,984)	(63,412)	(49,344)
Net cash flow	(355,452)	380,554	869,566	701,079	208,873	(57,479)	(230,669)	(291,929)	(245,257)	28,026	73,727	(445,471)	635,569
Ending cash balance	$376,232	$756,786	$1,626,352	$2,327,431	$2,536,304	$2,478,825	$2,248,156	$1,956,228	$1,710,971	$1,738,997	$1,812,724	$1,367,253	$1,367,253

Figure 5-24
DAYS SALES OUTSTANDING (DSO)

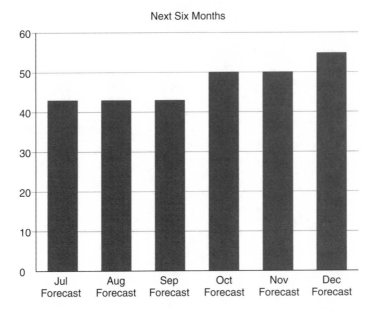

Next Six Months

negative net cash flow this year is the increase in accounts receivable associated with the assumption that DSO will go up near the end of the year as ABC brings on new, larger customers. This temporary slowdown in cash created the need to reduce the usual level of owner distributions and only pay the normal debt service requirements.

Figures 5-24 and 5-25 show a graph of DSO (Days Sales Outstanding) for the next six months and for the next year. The move up to, and above, the 50-day level in the fourth quarter of the current year is the key driver of the negative cash flow in the forecast (and the corresponding weaker cash balances).

Once the CEO had a view of what was likely to happen after contracting with the new (and much larger) customers, the discussion shifted to ways to mitigate the potential negative impact on cash and how to handle a cash shortage if the actuals came in *worse* than the forecast. That discussion focused on three steps:

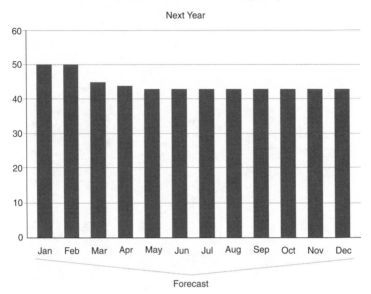

Figure 5-25
DAYS SALES OUTSTANDING (DSO)

Next Year

Forecast

1. Do everything we can to influence the speed of payment so invoices are paid in accordance with the contract terms. The primary insight here was that they would focus on "expediting" rather than "collecting" accounts receivable with the new customers. Management and accounting would meet with new customers long before the first invoice was issued in order to learn exactly how the customer's approval and payment process worked. The goal was to adhere to the new, larger customers' established accounts payable process and provide them everything they needed and in the format they required. That way ABC was doing its part to help ensure invoices would move through the accounts payable process without delay.

2. Meet with the bank in the coming weeks to walk the lenders through the forecast and make them aware that ABC may need to draw on the bank line between November and February. If

ABC did draw on the line, they expected to have it paid back in full by April.

3. Closely monitor financial results (especially accounts receivable and cash) in the coming months and meet regularly to review the steps being taken to mitigate the negative impact of a higher DSO.

This is a great example of how the forecasting process can create insight *and* action. Management and accounting have now created a *proactive* plan that will dramatically increase the likelihood of successfully onboarding these new customers/projects. This is because the forecast put a spotlight on the potential impact on cash once the new projects begin. Without the forecast, there would have been little thought put into these topics until the very last minute. At that point it would create an emergency and management would scramble to get the cash they need from the bank. Credibility would suffer and the company as a whole would have been in a weaker position as a result.

Show Historical and Forecast Results Side-by-Side

The financial model was set up to easily present the monthly forecast next to the monthly actual results. It could be shown on a calendar year basis and a trailing (and forward-looking) basis. This is an impactful way to make trends and direction obvious to the reader. One of the added benefits of this approach is that management becomes more knowledgeable about the financial statements and therefore more likely to pay closer attention to the numbers and trends each month.

Make the Forecast Part of Your Monthly Financial Rhythm

This final step in the process is what creates lasting value in the company. An updated forecast was included in the monthly reporting package every month going forward. The process was created so the last actual month was loaded and the forecast months updated with new information. The cover memo that was included in the monthly reporting package included a paragraph on key changes in the forecast. And, specific comments were included each month about how the company was doing on the two key focus areas with respect to cash: the impact of a higher DSO on owner distributions and ABC's ability to pay down debt faster. Shortly after receiving the monthly reporting package, the CEO and the board could quickly see what mattered most.

The 10 Rules for Creating a Forecast You Can Trust

Because the company was implementing a forecast process for the first time, we paid very close attention to the 10 rules for creating a forecast you can trust.

Here's how we wove the 10 rules into our implementation.

1. **It's all about decision making, not precision.** Our written objectives made it clear that the purpose of the forecast was to support a robust financial planning and monthly monitoring process for the board. The forecast would help provide a clear view of likely financial results in order to evaluate various growth plans and strategies. The forecast was all about strategic decision making. And we avoided the "precision trap" by speaking in the 2-minute summary in terms of a range of results rather than a single number. The summary included a sentence that said taxable income was expected to be in the range of $1.5 to $1.7 million in the current year and $2.2 to $2.5 million for next year. We consistently spoke in terms of the strategic impact of the forecast results and where the company was headed financially.

Figure 5-26
10 RULES FOR CREATING A FORECAST YOU CAN TRUST

1.	It's all about decision making, not precision
2.	Think top-down, not bottom-up
3.	Model a full set of financial statements
4.	First look back, then look forward
5.	Understand the high-level company strategy and expectations
6.	Simplify, simplify, simplify
7.	Create a repeatable process
8.	Be conservative
9.	Condense the results to a 2-minute summary
10.	Start for your eyes only

2. **Think top-down, not bottom-up.** One of the hardest things for an entrepreneur or CFO to do when creating a financial forecast is to avoid the tendency to gather assumptions at the lowest level and roll them up. It would have been very natural for the CFO to go to each of the company's project managers and ask them for very specific forecasts of how each job would progress toward completion and create a job-by-job accumulation of estimates and roll them up into the forecast. We avoided that by implementing a process where only two people were involved in making the forecast assumptions. We created our assumptions at the highest possible level based on our bigger picture discussions with management and our intuition and knowledge of the business.

3. **Model a full set of financial statements.** The forecast included a full set of financial statements (income statement, balance sheet, and statement of cash flows) in the same format ABC used for their monthly financial reporting. That way we could easily present the forecast results side-by-side with actual results

119

so trends and direction jumped off the page for the CEO and the board. We also included a summary view of the statement of cash flows to help make it much easier for everyone to understand the key drivers of cash flow each month.

4. **First look back, then look forward.** Our starting point, before considering any forecast assumptions, was to load the full set of financial statements for each of the last eighteen months. We calculated and reviewed each key financial driver over that eighteen month period in the same format as the forecast assumptions sheet that we would use for the forecast. That way we had a very clear view of what was driving results in the recent past.

5. **Understand the high-level company strategy and expectations.** Because the CFO was very involved in the business and was intimately familiar with the construction projects and their status, the work was more straightforward than in many companies. Most of our discussions were with the CEO about the future and his plans for growing and expanding the business. Some of the key forecast assumptions (and key insights about future financial results) came from the implications related to bidding on projects outside of their specialty area (with much larger customers than ABC had worked with in the past).

6. **Simplify, simplify, simplify.** One of the larger challenges in forecasting is to avoid complexity (and detail) - especially for a CFO. A CFO spends so much time creating and reviewing historical financial statements that it can be difficult to switch gears. Historical financial statements are created by gathering and recording detailed transactions and rolling them up into financial statements. The forecast is just the opposite because we are creating financial statements based on a dozen or so high-level drivers. In forecasting a full set of financial statements, the more detail you bring into the forecasting process, the more error you will create. We had frequent discussions

along the way to help us avoid the pitfall of diving down too far into the weeds.

7. **Create a repeatable process.** In our written objectives, we stated that we would incorporate the forecast into the monthly financial reporting process for the board. That meant we would need to be able to drop historical financial statements in the financial model each month and update the forecast months as well. And we would need to accomplish it without creating a lot of manual labor or creating a process that took too much time to complete each month. We built the financial model from the very beginning with repeatability in mind.

8. **Be conservative.** There is a natural tendency for a CEO who will be presenting a forecast to the board to be a bit too rosy in the forecast assumptions. It is human nature for CEOs and entrepreneurs to present grand plans and assume the plans will come together without a hitch. This happens to CFOs sometimes as well. Part of my role in the process was to coach and guide the CFO and the CEO on the appropriate use of conservativism in the assumptions (rather than being more aggressive) so the forecast represented what was most likely to happen (even if everything did not go as planned). Our assumption about DSO going higher in the fourth quarter related to ABC's expectation that the new, larger company projects will pay slower than its typical customers, was a result of a purposeful attempt to be conservative about how these larger customers might pay slower than existing customers.

9. **Condense the results to a 2-minute summary.** In our 2-minute summary we quickly hit the most important and impactful conclusions. We provided a range for profitability and pointed out that existing plans for owner distributions and paying down debt would be negatively impacted by the growth plans. Then we explained why that was likely to happen. All in a very short, here's what's likely to happen, 2-minute summary. And we were

prepared to support that summary by answering questions that the CEO and the board had.

10. **Start for your eyes only.** Because we were implementing the forecast for the first time at ABC, we made the first few attempts (drafts) "for our eyes only." In this case, the CFO and I "test drove" the forecast for a short while as we worked out the kinks and proved to ourselves that we had created a reliable financial forecasting process. Only after we confirmed that we had the process working properly did we begin sharing the forecast results with the CEO and the board.

Note: I have combined several experiences with business owners into this example. It is based on the last in a series of three articles I wrote for the Construction Financial Management Association (CFMA) *Building Profits* magazine. (Copyright © 2016 by the Construction Financial Management Association (CFMA). All rights reserved. This article first appeared in the January/February 2016 issue of *CFMA Building Profits* and is reprinted with permission.) A link to each of the three articles (and the full spreadsheet version of the financial model for ABC) is in the free resources section of the Financial Rhythm website that supports this book at www.ILove-Forecasting.com.

PART THREE

How to Overcome the Obstacles to Forecasting

"If you want to teach people a new way of thinking, don't bother trying to teach them. Instead, give them a tool, the use of which will lead to new ways of thinking."

—*R. Buckminster Fuller,*
Designer, inventor,
futurist

Chapter 6

Choosing Your Software Tool–Spreadsheets vs. Forecasting Software

"If all you have is a hammer, everything looks like a nail."

—ABRAHAM MASLOW

Forecasting tools generally fall into two categories: homegrown spreadsheets (usually in Excel) and forecasting software. Of course, spreadsheets are a common tool for all things financial. Creating a forecast in Excel can work well in a company with spreadsheet "power users," analysts on staff to create and maintain the financial model, or an organization that prefers "roll your own" solutions to acquiring software from outside vendors. Spreadsheets can be fully customized and are relatively inexpensive to get started.

However, spreadsheets are not ideal for a company that prefers a more robust and lasting solution or one in which a complex legal entity consolidation is required to present consolidated actual and forecast results. Spreadsheets can become clunky and difficult to maintain over time, involve a lot of manual input, and are prone to human error unless significant time is spent managing and expanding the financial model. In addition, the underlying logic for modeling a full set of financial statements is complex and must be developed and working properly before you can begin the actual forecasting work.

Forecasting software is specialized, dynamic, and built for large amounts of data as well as the ability to import data and perform complex reporting. However, it can be a costly solution that requires professional assistance and extra time to set up and maintain. Figure 6-1 shows the benefits and downsides of each.

Figure 6-1
SPREADSHEETS VS. SOFTWARE

Homegrown Spreadsheets	
BENEFITS	**DOWNSIDES**
Easy to get started quickly	Underlying financial model must be created
Ease of use if you are proficient with spreadsheets	Robust reporting capability must be created
Customization of the drivers, assumptions, and the look and feel	Manual entry of data in some cases
No new software to install or learn	Forecast periods must be regularly added to the model
No reliance on an outside vendor	Can become clunky and difficult to maintain over time
Inexpensive to get started	Complexity goes up as data is added
	Prone to human error

Forecasting Software	
BENEFITS	**DOWNSIDES**
Handles the underlying complexity of the financial model	Software must be purchased and learned
Handles the reporting of historical and forecast periods	Requires professional assistance to implement in many cases
Built on a database that can handle the accumulation of data	Takes longer to get your forecast process up and running
Ability to do multi-entity consolidations and reporting	Time and costs increase when customization is required
Ability to import data electronically	
Promotes a more repeatable forecasting process	

Whichever way you go, the software you build or choose for forecasting should:

- Include the underlying logic for forecasting (or modeling) a full set of financial statements.
- Provide the ability to forecast with financial and nonfinancial data.
- Import historical (actual) financial results.
- Present both historical and forecast results in reports, report packages, and exports.
- Display graphical views of data and trends (this is a powerful feature for communicating insight).
- Be easy to update and maintain each month.
- Make your monthly financial reporting process simple and fast.

FORECASTING SOFTWARE

I'm one of those financial guys who believes that spreadsheets are essential to business . . . but they are also a bit overused. It's the old saying that when all you have is a hammer, everything starts to look like a nail. Most of the time I spend in spreadsheets is focused on trying to simplify something. And building and maintaining a financial model over time is the opposite of simplification (at least for me because I'm not a spreadsheet power user).

There are many planning and forecasting applications on the market. Many of the high-end enterprise resource planning (ERP) and corporate performance management (CPM) systems include robust forecasting capabilities. These are generally expensive and used by large companies with large budgets. (By large company I'm referring to greater than $500 million in revenues.) There are also tools that can work well in large companies as well as medium to smaller businesses. Those include:

- SurvivalWare
- PlanGuru
- Hyperion
- Adaptive Insights
- Prophix
- Host Analytics
- Budget Maestro
- bi360
- Tagetik
- . . . and many more

My personal experience with these tools is almost exclusively with SurvivalWare because I have been using it for the last twelve years. (As a result, I have had limited need to explore or evaluate other forecasting tools.) So, my specific comments and insights about forecasting tools will be based on my experience and knowledge of SurvivalWare. I'll also share some information about PlanGuru based on input from a super-bright CPA who owns and manages an accounting firm that caters to the accounting needs of U.S. based law firms. But all the forecasting tools are worth researching before you make your decision about which tool is best for your needs and for your company.

SurvivalWare – My Forecasting Tool of Choice

SurvivalWare is a powerful financial analysis and forecasting tool. I have used it for small and large companies, single entity and multi-entity companies, and multi-location franchise and non-franchise businesses across a wide variety of industries. I value the underlying financial model that is built for forecasting as well as its strong financial analysis, graphing, and reporting capabilities.

Rusty Luhring is the founder of Luhring SurvivalWare, Inc. and the genius behind the SurvivalWare application. Rusty spent twenty years creating sophisticated, customized financial models for large organizations including Marriott, Texaco, Federal Express, and

128

many others. Back in 2000, he decided to bring the sophisticated financial modeling technology used for large corporations to small and medium-sized companies. He recognized that smaller companies needed access to an affordable way to create forecasts and projections. He created SurvivalWare to put a powerful planning and analysis tool into the hands of companies who needed it even more so than large companies.

SurvivalWare is a windows-based program that is heavily graphical and comes with a simplified user interface. It is delivered with two off the shelf corporate planning models pre-built. You can also engage SurvivalWare consultants to create customized planning models and analysis systems that can be run by non-technical business owners and financial staff or advisors using the SurvivalWare platform.

Multi-Location, Multi-Entity Company. One client of Survival-Ware had multiple legal entities and was using spreadsheets as their consolidation and financial reporting tool. The owner wanted to put more focus on the key drivers of performance and she wanted a forecast so she could begin planning and working on driving profitability higher. She created a profitability forecast for each entity and then had it rolled up in order to see the consolidated view of results in addition to the entity level view. The project took her a long time to complete in her homegrown spreadsheet.

Then she realized that it was impossible to maintain each month. It turned out to be a one-time exercise because it could not be turned into a repeatable process each month. Not only that, but the spreadsheet version only included the income statement. There was no forecast for the balance sheet and cash flow. The complexity of forecasting a full set of financial statements was way beyond the capability of her homegrown spreadsheet approach.

With the help of SurvivalWare, and customizing it to the specific needs of her business model, she was able to implement a powerful tool that simplified the monthly forecasting and management process for her multi-location and multi-entity business. It put the focus on the key drivers of performance and helped turn the monthly financial information into a fantastic decision-making tool for her and her investors.

Unique Capabilities for Franchise Companies. Another very unique capability of SurvivalWare is how it can be used by a franchise company. In years past, I was a CFO of an international franchisor where I came to understand a fascinating problem that exists in the franchise world. Everyone in franchising knows that the success of a franchise company ultimately comes down to financial performance at the location/franchisee level. Yet, the vast majority of franchisors don't have location-level profitability and cash flow numbers. They have no effective way of providing financial rankings, comparisons and benchmarks to their franchisees across the key performance measures that determine profitability and cash flow at the location level. Most franchisees have no fact-based, consistent way to compare their monthly financial results to best practices or overall averages so they can focus on the areas most in need of improvement.

Any business with hundreds of company-owned locations would have complete financial data on those stores to manage and compare. But virtually no franchise company has that same level of financial information. There are franchise systems with hundreds of franchisees running very similar businesses yet they don't have frequent, comparative, action oriented financial data so each franchisee knows exactly where they stand on the critical drivers of financial success at the location level. As a result, most franchisees are starving for easy-to-understand comparisons and benchmarks on key performance measures. It was true in the 1990s . . . and it's still true in many franchise companies today.

SurvivalWare solved that problem for a number of popular, respected franchise companies with hundreds of locations across the

U.S. Many of the features that make SurvivalWare a strong financial analysis and forecasting tool were ideally suited to the challenges of a multi-location franchise system. It provided the unique ability to:

- Allow the electronic import of a full set of financial statements from every franchisee automatically, regardless of the accounting system the franchisee used and regardless of their chart of accounts.
- Allow the electronic import of nonfinancial data from point-of-sale systems and other data sources in order to calculate the key drivers and metrics of financial performance.
- Automatically convert each franchisee's financial statements into a common format. The system uses an internal "map" from the franchisee's chart of accounts to the franchisors common chart of accounts. This allows them to import a full set of financial and nonfinancial data every month.
- Provide the ability to review and distribute a full set of financial and operating rankings, benchmarks, and best practices based on the key performance measures that drive profitability and cash flow at the location level.
- Give franchisees a graphical dashboard view into those same key performance measures for the last 24 to 36 months to help them understand and manage their cash flow in a way impossible from their accounting system.
- Make it possible for the franchisee and/or the franchisor to create a reliable financial forecast down to the cash flow level.

Now the franchisor could finally bring the key performance measures and detailed financial results from across the system to their franchisees in an easy-to-understand, clear, and consistent format. The software made it possible for the franchisor to sort, filter, analyze, and present the key drivers of financial results across their entire system. Franchisees could quickly and easily see the dollar value of improving any of the key metrics and quantify how much money they could put to their bottom line by improving in that specific performance category.

Paul Carlson, CPA, Uses PlanGuru

Paul Carlson is a CPA who owns and operates a unique accounting firm that caters to the accounting needs of U.S. based law firms. Paul uses PlanGuru to provide a reliable financial forecast for clients as part of his fractional Controller and CFO services. This service is designed for growing businesses that reach a point where they require the guidance of a Controller or CFO, but are not large enough to support a full-time position. His part-time Controller and CFO service provides the needed guidance for clients without the price tag of a full-time employee. Paul's firm goes above and beyond providing financial statements and tax returns for clients by helping law firms proactively manage and improve the financial side of their business. He uses financial forecasts to help his law firm clients:

- Avoid cash surprises.
- Provide a financial road map the partners can use to guide and manage the firm.
- Establish goals and measure financial and nonfinancial progress toward those goals.
- Provide the managing partners a way to document their partner distribution expectations.
- More clearly understand the difference between profits and cash flow.
- Closely link business decisions to the financial and cash flow implications of those decisions.

Paul has been using PlanGuru for five years. It is a database driven financial modeling tool that helps reduce formulas and assumption errors and provides the ability to forecast a full set of financial statements (including cash flow). Paul uses the "supporting schedules" feature so he can forecast payroll costs down to the employee level to make it easier for clients to understand the numbers. (He has found this very helpful in working with his law firm clients.) PlanGuru provides what Paul describes as "clean control" of the key forecast assumptions. He also likes the ratio analysis reports and the ability to provide a scorecard that summarizes the key financial indicators for his client and helps provide the monthly feedback they need to continue to grow and improve their business.

You can learn more about Paul Carlson and his accounting firm at lawfirmvelocity.com and pcarlsoncpa.com.

The Case for Spreadsheets

I mentioned earlier that one reason I don't use spreadsheets more often is that I am *not* a spreadsheet power user. For some reason that skill has alluded me over the years. But there are lots of spreadsheet power users out there who can turn a spreadsheet into an incredibly powerful tool for financial forecasting and analysis.

Meet James H. Johnson, CPA, of the accounting firm Trainer, Wright, & Paterno CPAs in Huntington, West Virginia. James is a power user extraordinaire who can work magic with a spreadsheet. He works in the firm's consulting practice (TWP Consulting), where he specializes in helping manufacturing and construction companies turn numbers and data into insight and financial improvement. Much of his work revolves around helping CEOs understand the forward-looking view of financial performance while also doing a much deeper dive into operational performance metrics and day-to-day improvement opportunities. This is where his advanced systems knowledge shines when building and maintaining complex spreadsheets.

James uses ODBC and other database connectivity tools to connect directly to a company's Enterprise Resource Planning (ERP) system from within his spreadsheet models. In a construction company, he would use these tools to bring in work in process details like committed costs, final agreed upon price, and other data points relevant to decision making. In a manufacturing company, he might auto-populate detailed manufacturing and SKU level data to help management make very specific operational and manufacturing decisions. He merges his knowledge of accounting and technology to build spreadsheets that can be used every month to help a company fine-tune their decision making at both the strategic planning level as well as the day-to-day operational level.

You can learn more about James and the firm at www.twpcpa.com.

GETTING STARTED

Chances are you are going to want (or need) someone to help you get your forecasting process up and running. Talk to your CFO, your controller, your CPA, or another outside resource experienced in using forecasts as a monthly tool for decision making. They will likely have a tool of choice that they regularly use for forecasts. They may have even created sophisticated financial models in spreadsheets designed to "plug and play" for their clients. Either way, the benefit for you is that you won't have to make the decision yourself about which tool is best. Just make sure you talk with them about the benefits and downsides of the tool they prefer (or suggest).

If you have a hard time lining up the resources to help you, send me an email at pcampbell@financialrhythm.com or pcampbellcfo@gmail.com and I will happily point you in the right direction.

Chapter 7

The Most Common Forecasting "Yes, buts . . ."

"Anything worth doing well is worth doing poorly at first."

—Brian Tracy

A "yes, but" happens when you say, "Yes Philip, that's a great idea. I really should have a clear view through the financial windshield of my business. I agree I need to create a reliable financial forecast, but . . . what about . . . and what about . . .?"

Basically, you agree with what needs to be done (create a financial forecasting process in your business), but something is preventing you from actually doing it. You have a worry or concern that is keeping you from taking action right now. A "yes, but" is a natural result of thinking through the implications of trying something new. So let's dive into those obstacles and see if we can remove them as roadblocks.

Yes, but . . .: My board is not asking for a forecast each month. They seem to be happy with what we already provide in the way of financial statements. Why should I introduce a forecast into the mix if they are not asking for it?

Answer: I love this question because the same thing went through my head years ago as a young CFO. I have been the CFO in several companies where, at least in the early days, the CEO and the board were not asking me for a forecast. I even tried convincing them of the value of having a forecast, but without much luck. I implemented the forecast process *anyway*. Then I evaluated how the forecast helped *me*. It helped me become even more knowledgeable about our business model. I discovered some pitfalls in our growth strategy and proactively worked to shed light on the issue and improve the strategy. The forecast also helped me when I reviewed the financial statements each month because I could compare actual results to my expectation. It helped me spot errors in the financials in a matter of minutes without even diving down into the transaction level details.

After a short while, the CEO and the board began to see that my knowledge of the business and where the company was going financially was growing every month. They were surprised that I could "predict" certain things well before they happened. It was an eye-opening experience for me. It sealed in my mind the value of a reliable financial forecast. It even helped me make more money as a CFO and increase my ownership position in the company (that one really got my attention). And they became believers in the value of the view through the financial windshield of the business.

A reliable financial forecast is one of the most powerful tools you can use to grow your business successfully.

Start the process for your eyes only. Then work on selling the board on its value only after you have seen the value firsthand.

Yes, but . . .: My business is unpredictable. How can I know exactly what's about to happen financially? What if my forecast is wrong?

Answer: Remember, the question isn't whether your financial forecast is *wrong*. It's whether your forecast is *reliable*. You have an expectation of what you are trying to achieve in your business. You have a plan you are working every month to drive financial results. There is no question the forecast will be wrong (from a precision perspective). The critical question is whether it helps you make better, more informed financial and strategic decisions as you execute your plan.

Precision is the enemy when it comes to creating a reliable financial forecast.

As a longtime CPA and CFO, I understand the almost hardwired concern about being right when it comes to providing financial information. The single biggest step you can take to overcome the fear of being wrong is to create your first forecast . . . but don't share it with anyone yet. That's rule #10 for creating a financial forecast you can trust. This rule helps you get your forecast process started (which is half the battle in starting anything new). And you eliminate any criticism if it isn't perfect because no one will even see it at first.

This is a common sense, logical method that I have used with great success over the years. It overcomes our natural tendency toward inertia when starting something new and it eliminates the fear of being wrong. The beauty of getting started on your first "for your eyes only" forecast is you get to taste the benefits without worrying at all about what others might think or if your numbers might be "wrong." You are giving yourself permission to learn and experiment at this beginning stage. Even without sharing the forecast results initially, you still get to experience the benefits of the financial forecasting process. The benefits enable you to:

- Become intimately familiar with the strategy and direction of your company.
- Identify the key drivers of financial performance.
- Reduce the risk of error in the historical financial statements.
- Compare actuals to forecast each month to learn which parts of your forecasting process are working well and which need some work or fine tuning.
- Create insights about past and future financial performance.
- Think through ways to simplify the forecast process.
- Consider the best way to present the forecast when the time is right so that it is simple and easy to understand.

After running the forecast process for three months, you will become much more confident and knowledgeable about the numbers and the forecast approach. You will know firsthand where the landmines are that you need to avoid. You will have a better sense of the kinds of strategic and monthly decisions that the forecast can influence and help improve.

> "Everything we have been taught conditions us to believe that right answers are good and wrong answers are bad, yet when faced with developing a forecast, the odds are stacked against us. Getting over the fear of being wrong is the first step toward developing a best practice forecasting process."
>
> —David Axson, *Best Practices in Planning and Performance Management: From Data to Decisions*

Remember to use a range of likely financial outcomes when providing estimates of profitability and certain balance sheet amounts.

It helps you put some "guardrails" around what you think should happen financially while leaving yourself some room for error or surprise once the actual results come in.

Yes, but...: I am launching a new business so I don't have any historical results to look back at. How do I forecast when I don't have any historical data?

Answer: When you are starting a business, creating a new division within your company, or otherwise launching something new, you can't "First look back, then look forward" as forecasting rule #4 says. There are no historical financial results to look back on. But you do have at least some glimmer of an *expectation* for your new venture. And a forecast is basically an expectation of what you believe is about to happen financially. So you want to explore those expectations and do your forecasting based on a range of possibilities and your current thinking on how things might unfold from a financial perspective.

Here are three tips that will help you as you begin the work of turning your expectations (and a range of possible outcomes) into a reliable financial forecast.

First, remember that one of the benefits of forecasting is that it helps you to better understand your business model. You already have a good sense for what kind of business or venture you are launching. Now you want to "put some numbers to it." The process of creating different versions of a forecast will help you learn what the key financial and nonfinancial drivers of performance are. It will force you to think deeply about what makes your new venture tick. It will help you find the "levers" that can move the needle and help it to be successful.

As you move further along in making specific assumptions about financial performance, the process will force you to ask some tough questions. "Can we really add new customers at the rate I am projecting over the next twelve months? How much will we have to increase operating expenses to achieve the plan? How fast can a salesperson

139

bring on new customers in order to cover their salary and overhead costs?" The process forces you to look hard for any weak links in your strategy. You will discover some powerful insights about your business model as you become more intimately familiar with what will really drive financial performance and make the new venture a success.

Second, another benefit I talked about in Chapter 2 was that a forecast is the ideal tool for exercising your leadership muscles. You will need other people to help you make the new business or venture successful. A forecast will help you paint a picture for your management team and others of what your vision and goals for this new venture look like financially. What does it look like if it goes well? What does it look like if it does not go well? What are the metrics that matter most? You want to create a range of possibilities so you know what success or failure could look like. It helps you put some "guardrails" around what you think should happen financially. It helps you communicate your vision in a more concrete way than just talking about it without having the financial picture to go with it.

Third, remember that the forecasting process will help you anticipate the financial implications of growth. Growth, especially rapid growth, is almost always a net user of cash in the early days. Many executives are caught by surprise when they are successful in a new business or venture only to grow their way right into a cash crisis. They end up running to the bank and begging on bended knee for a line of credit or an increase on their existing line of credit. That hurts your credibility. The forecasting process will help you to more fully understand the financial and cash flow implications of achieving your growth plans.

Yes, but...: If my primary objective is to forecast cash flow, would it be easier to use a receipts and disbursements approach rather than modeling a full set of accrual basis financial statements?

Answer: Forecasting cash flow using a cash in and cash out approach can be dangerous because it is so easy to create an *unreliable* cash flow forecast. Having said that, there are certain circumstances where I would use that approach…but I would not do it in place of modeling a full set of financial statements. I would do it *in addition to modeling a full set of financial statements.*

If you are in the middle of a cash crisis, then creating and maintaining a weekly cash flow forecast can be helpful. If you are struggling to pay lenders, vendors are raising hell and demanding answers about when they will be paid, or if you are experiencing similar "the house is on fire" kinds of cash problems, a weekly cash flow forecast should be added to your toolkit in addition to your monthly forecasting.

But be very careful because a cash in and cash out kind of weekly forecast doesn't have the benefits of being done "inside the four walls" of the financial statements. It is super easy to create estimates that are hard to double check and hard to monitor (and easy to mess up). One tip for the wise with weekly cash flow forecasts—make sure you use a format where you drop actual cash flow results into the schedule as soon as the week is over. That is the single most important step you can take to help ensure the cash flow forecast is based on reality and avoid creating a big bust in your forecast.

Yes, but. . .: I don't really understand financial statements, at least not intimately. Can I create a reliable forecast with only a limited understanding of financial statements?

Answer: One of the many benefits of starting the forecasting process is you will very quickly learn how financial statements work, either by getting the process started yourself or by having someone help you or run the process for you. If you don't feel comfortable with financial statements, I suggest you use that as a sign that beginning the forecast process is even more important for you. Reach out to some people who can help you get started. Your understanding of the business will skyrocket as a result.

> "I found accounting nearly impossible to learn because of the bubbling moat of boredom that surrounds the entire field.
>
> But a basic understanding of accounting is necessary to be a fully effective adult in a modern society, even if you never do any actual accounting on your own.
>
> ...Accounting is part of the vocabulary of business, and if you don't understand it on a concept level, the world will be a confusing place.
>
> ...You can pay others to do your accounting and cash-flow projections, but that only works if you can check their work in a meaningful way. The smarter play is to learn enough about accounting and spreadsheets that you understand the basics."
>
> —Scott Adams (the creator of "Dilbert"),
> Author, *How to Fail at Almost Everything and Still Win Big*

Yes, but. . .: My financial statements are a mess. I don't know exactly what's wrong. I just know I can't rely on them. Will that create a problem in the forecasting process?

Answer: The short answer is Yep, that will create a problem! It's the old garbage in, garbage out saying. The beginning point for creating a reliable financial forecast is accurate and reliable financial statements. I believe in fast, accurate, and insightful financial statements and financial information. In my view, business is hard enough, making money is hard enough, without tying one hand behind your back and praying everything turns out okay. Step one in this case is to sit down with the person(s) responsible for the accuracy and timeliness of your financial statements and talk about the importance of reliable financial statements and find out what's wrong. Then make it very clear that you expect the problem to be fixed and that you will do what it takes to support them in getting the work done. Don't allow your accounting function to produce financial statements that are slow and sloppy.

Yes, but . . .: I have tried forecasting before but couldn't get reliable estimates and projections from the people in charge of sales.

Answer: This is a common mistake when beginning the forecasting process. The natural tendency is to go deep into the organization and ask people to make estimates and projections so you can accumulate their projections and roll them up into your forecast. But remember, the process I teach in this book is to go at the forecast as a top-down, not a bottom-up process. Although creating historical financial statements is a bottom-up process of gathering and recording transactions and reporting the results in the form of accurate financial statements, creating a financial forecast is a top-down exercise.

You must take yourself up to the 30,000-foot level and look down on the business financially as you forecast. It's about painting a picture of what the financial results will likely be based on your knowledge and intuition rather than rolling up a series of detailed estimates or projections.

For example, as I shared earlier, when forecasting revenues, you should ask yourself this question: What two numbers could I multiply together to arrive at revenues?

- For a retailer, it might be number of customers × average ticket = revenues.
- For a law firm, it might be hours incurred by attorneys × average billing rate = revenues.
- For a wholesaler of fuel, it might be gallons of fuel sold × average selling price per gallon = revenues.

Your forecast looks at the strategic view and direction of where the company is going – not the nitty-gritty bottom-up details.

Yes, but. . .: I don't have time to create and maintain a monthly forecast. And I don't feel like I have the staff that can do it either.

Answer: In my book, *Never Run Out of Cash: The 10 Cash Flow Rules You Can't Afford to Ignore*, I talked about the principle that when something important needs to be done in your business, you must either do the work yourself. . . or have someone do it for you. Flying blind is a bad option. Driving along on the highway of business without a clear view through your financial windshield is unwise. The better option is to either begin learning what it takes to create a reliable financial forecast or to reach out to people who can do all, or some, of the work for you. Talk to your CFO, your controller, your outside CPA, or other consultants. Ask other entrepreneurs for input on resources and professionals that can help you get started.

If you have a hard time lining up the resources to help you, send me an email at pcampbell@financialrhythm.com or pcampbellcfo@gmail.com and I will happily point you in the right direction.

> "For anything to change, someone has to start acting differently."
>
> —Chip Heath and Dan Heath, *Switch: How to Change Things When Change Is Hard*

Your Next Step

As I end this chapter on how to overcome the obstacles to forecasting, I'd like to share a cool story and some insightful tips from a fantastic book. The book is *Future Ready: How to Master Business Forecasting*. It is written by two of the leading experts in performance management, Steve Morlidge and Steve Player.

They tell a great story on pages 10 and 11 about a meeting of the Beyond Budgeting Round Table in New York (Steve Player is the North American Program Director for the Beyond Budgeting Round Table). One of the top financial analysts on Wall Street was going to speak to the group about what he looks for from a company regarding a view into where their business is headed. Here is the short version from the book:

> "If you are in charge of a business and can't tell me what is going to happen at the end of the quarter then I suspect that you don't know what you are doing. On the other hand, if you can tell me exactly what is going to happen in a year's time then you are either a fool or a liar.
>
> . . . It is a common misconception among managers that 'Wall Street' demands that businesses accurately predict the future. This view simply does not stand up to scrutiny.
>
> . . . What I, as an experienced analyst, want from you is a projection with some ranges around it, a good idea of what is driving the uncertainty and a convincing plan of how you are going to mitigate the risk or exploit the opportunity. I can then do something you can't do; I can go and ask your competitors the same question and based on that I will make the judgment about whether you are a good investment or not."

They go on to say:

> "So, according to this knowledgeable source, the market doesn't demand that you predict the future. It does expect that you have a good grasp of what might happen and are well prepared to deal with it. Isn't that just good, common sense?"

Think about that for a minute in your own business.

- Do you understand your business enough to create a forecast of what is likely to happen in the coming months?
- Can you identify the areas of uncertainty that your management team will have to deal with to hit your targets?
- Do you have a plan for mitigating the risks that could derail your plans?

145

- How are you going to exploit opportunities to improve your profitability and cash flow?

And one final quote that is very important about forecasts:

> "We argue that we do not need accuracy from a forecast process—we need reliability. By reliability, we mean forecasts that are accurate enough for our purpose: decision-making."

Go for It

That's a great reminder that forecasts are all about helping you make better business decisions. What better time than right now to put the power of a reliable financial forecast to work in your business. It will change the way you grow and manage your business forever.

Go for it!

Chapter 8

The Secret to Driving Growth, Profitability, and Cash Flow Higher

"The whole aim of starting a business is to develop a consistent, predictable source of cash flow in excess of cost and expenses and then to hold on to the money."

—BRIAN TRACY

My ultimate goal in this book is to help you improve your profitability and cash flow. I would get such a kick out of knowing that I helped you in some small way to grow an exciting company that takes good care of you financially (not the other way around). I would absolutely love to see you create a net worth in the millions and turn your hard work and persistence into true and lasting financial success.

Of course, financial forecasting isn't going to magically drive your revenues higher or your expenses lower overnight. Financial forecasting is a *tool*…and a *thought process*. Improving profitability and cash flow takes *action*. But your forecast will:

- Point you to the key drivers that matter most (so you know where to focus).
- Shine a light on the opportunities for increasing your profits and cash flow (so you can take action).
- Help you make better, smarter financial decisions (so your actions create results).

To help you get those benefits as quickly and easily as possible, I designed the approach to financial forecasting I teach in this book with two key principles in mind. The first is that the hardest part of doing something new is getting started. That's why I created a process to help you get started quickly. You don't need expensive tools to get started. Learn the 10 rules, and then follow the recipe. Get started "for your eyes only" to prove to yourself that the forecasting process adds value. It is a fast and risk free way to get started.

Second, the forecasting process is designed as a big picture, top-down exercise to help you stay out of the weeds when creating your forecast. Once you create a clear view through the financial windshield at the overall level, *then* the specific drivers of performance that need your attention will jump out at you. As you paint the broader picture of financial performance, *then* you can drill down on the more detailed drivers of financial success that you need to act on.

Let me show you an example of how a financial forecast leads to specific actions that can help you improve profits and cash flow.

Shining the Light on Opportunity

A multi-unit retail chain was wrestling with a sales decline and debating ideas on how to fix it. They agreed that creating a financial forecast was step one so they could answer the question "What's about to happen?"

Comparable store sales are an important metric in retailing, and they had been falling recently. They were worried about it, so they asked the store managers and regional managers "What's going on?" The response from the field was, "Help, we need more customers. The corporate office needs to provide us with additional marketing to drive new customers in to the stores or this problem is going to get worse."

The management team at corporate knew they had a problem. They knew they had to do something about it. But the marketing budget was tight and they were uncomfortable just spending more money on marketing and blowing the budget.

Management agreed with me that the two numbers we could multiply together to get the monthly sales forecast was number of

Figure 8-1
CUSTOMER TRANSACTIONS

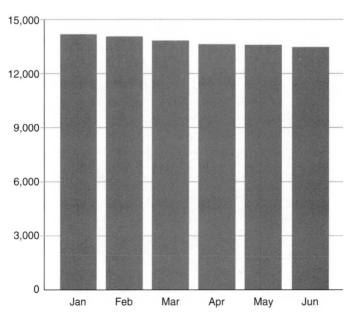

Figure 8-2
AVERAGE TICKET

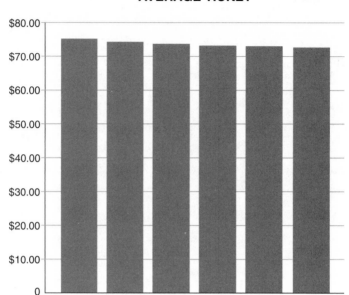

customer transactions times average ticket. So we gathered the actual results for the last six months for those two numbers and noticed some interesting trends. Figure 8-1 is a graph of customer transactions. Figure 8-2 is a graph of the average ticket.

At first glance, it appeared that the input from the field that they "need more customers" was accurate. The average ticket was down a bit but the number of customer transactions was way down. Absent information to the contrary, the forecast for the next three to six months was going to be a continuation of the decline in customer transactions and average ticket. That didn't sit well with the president. It showed a sales decline that was ripping a big hole in profitability. (One of the things I love about the forecasting process is it will get the attention of the owner or managers real fast when the forecast results aren't pretty!)

So we decided to drill down to the next level to see if we could learn more about what was driving the declining customer count. We asked the question again but in a little different way: "What two numbers can we multiply, or add, together to get customer transactions?" We agreed that the two numbers were (1) new customers plus (2) repeat customers = total customers. When a customer made a purchase, they were either a new customer or an existing customer (a repeat customer). So we went back to the point of sale system and gathered the recent history for new and repeat customer counts.

Figure 8-3 is a graph of new customers. Figure 8-4 is a graph of repeat customers.

The number of new customers making a purchase looked good and hadn't fallen off. But look at the number of repeat customers. It was going down in a significant way. The core problem wasn't lack of

Figure 8-3
NEW CUSTOMERS

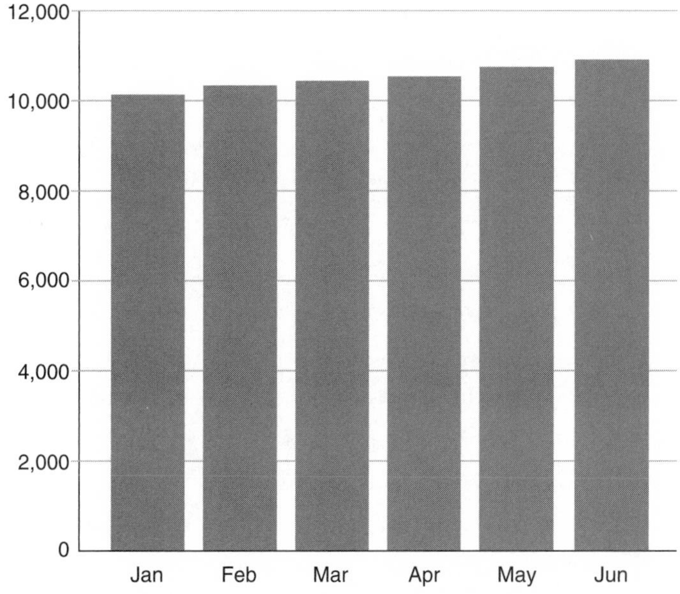

Figure 8-4
REPEAT CUSTOMERS

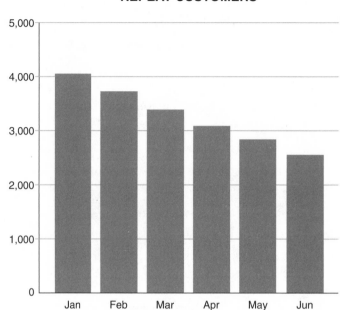

new customers. It was the fact that existing customers were not coming back to make purchases the way they had in the past. To make matters worse, repeat customers spent more than new customers on average, so they had a "double whammy" negative impact on sales.

This created an "aha" moment for management because now the action needed to address the problem was not what they thought at first—more advertising and marketing dollars to get new customers. The problem was totally different. The focus quickly shifted to finding out why existing customers were not coming back. The question was "Why are our existing customers abandoning us?" It could be many different issues causing existing customer visits to go down. But launching a marketing blitz to get new customers was definitely not the way to address it. In fact, driving a bunch of new customers into the store while the percentage of repeat purchases is dropping and can't be explained could be a very costly mistake.

Management created a series of initiatives designed to get feedback from existing customers, improve the in-store customer experience, create incentives and "bounce back" offers to stimulate repeat visits, train staff on providing a higher level of customer service, and renew the focus throughout the company on the importance of delighting customers. The forecasting process helped shine the light on the key drivers of results. And the follow-up work to drill down just a bit deeper helped management make a proper diagnosis of the problem. They were dangerously close to making a big financial mistake if they had just gone with their gut response to solving the problem of declining sales.

The example we walked through in Chapter 5 was very similar. The forecasting process led management to take proactive action to improve their customer and project onboarding process, change how they invoiced customers as projects progressed, and move their approach to accounts receivable from a collections mindset to an expediting mindset.

And it all started with creating a reliable financial forecast.

THE FORECAST LEADS TO ACTION

I love these examples because they highlight the power and purpose of forecasting. The forecasting process encourages you to identify and understand the key drivers of results at the highest level as you get started. As you think through and update the forecast, you begin to see the key drivers that need your attention. Then you drill down a layer or two on those key drivers to find out what actions you can take to improve profitability and cash flow. The forecasting tool and process shines the light on opportunities in a way that no other tool can. You will be surprised what it reveals for you once you get started.

Remember, your success in business will ultimately be determined by the degree to which you create, and hang on to, CASH.

Always working on ways to improve your profitability and cash flow is what creating cash is all about. You want your business to generate *excess* cash. At the end of the day that's what makes your business worth lots of money. And it's excess cash that will provide the distributions you need to grow your personal net worth by investing in income generating assets outside of your business.

Growing a business that is worth a lot of money *plus* creating a strong and growing personal net worth is your goal.

Riding along on the highway of business without a clear view through your financial windshield is foolish. You would never do that in your car, especially if your family was riding along with you. Why would you do it in your business when your financial future, and the financial future of your family, is riding on the success of your company?

Driving growth, profitability, and cash flow higher and higher is part of your mission. It has nothing to do with greed. It's all about making sure that you survive and thrive in business. A reliable financial forecast is a powerful tool to help you make that happen. And there's no better time than right now to get started!

> "A forecast should be our best estimate on the future, the expected outcome whether we like what we see or not. The purpose of a forecast is to get issues on the radar screen early enough to be able to take necessary actions. It is not necessarily about being right, but about being ready."
>
> Bjarte Bogsnes, *Implementing Beyond Budgeting: Unlocking the Performance Potential (Second Edition)*

What's *about to happen* in your business over the next few months?

What *could happen* in your business over the next six to eighteen months?

You owe it to yourself, and to everyone else who is depending on your financial success, to put a tool and a process in place so you always have the answers.

Good luck growing a fantastic, financially successful company. I'm rooting for you!

"Don't focus so hard on not paying taxes. Focus instead on increasing your profits."

Greg Crabtree,
Simple Numbers, Straight Talk, Big Profits!

Bonus Chapters

I have included two bonus chapters for you. It's my way of providing you a little freebie . . . a book within a book.

The first bonus chapter is a three-part plan for breathing financial life back into your business. It will give you a sensible plan, a roadmap, you can follow that will guide you on your path to building a business that takes care of you financially . . . not the other way around. This roadmap will guide you along the full financial life cycle of your business.

The second bonus chapter will help you evaluate your accounting and finance function, what some people consider a necessary evil, and turn it into an asset the financial community respects and admires and that forms the foundation for helping you grow and succeed financially. Too many entrepreneurs have a weak accounting and financial function in their business. It handcuffs their ability to grow and attract capital and talent. It hurts their credibility with bankers, lenders, investors, partners, and all those in the financial community you need to grow your business successfully.

I'll show you how to turn the accounting and financial function within your business into an important strategic asset. An asset that will help you win in business. An asset that will help you create confidence and credibility with all the people interested in, and invested in, the financial success of your company.

Bonus Chapter 1

A Three-Part Plan to Breathe Financial Life Back into Your Business

"The function of a business is to create money, not consume it, and the longer you postpone this the harder it gets to fix."

—Gary Sutton, *The Six-Month Fix*

In this bonus chapter, I'll show you a three-part plan for breathing financial life back into your business. It will give you a sensible plan, a roadmap, you can follow that will guide you on your path to building a strong, wealth generating business.

I like to look at the path to creating a company that is financially strong as a three-part, 10-step process that you see in Figure B1-1.

This plan is designed to guide you through the full financial life cycle of your business, and it has three parts.

- Part 1 is about confronting the financial reality of your business.
- Part 2 is about how you create a financial safety net within your business.
- Part 3 is how to go about the process of growing and enjoying financial success in your business.

Figure B1-1

BUILDING A FINANCIALLY STRONG BUSINESS

Keys you can apply today to promote solid financial growth!

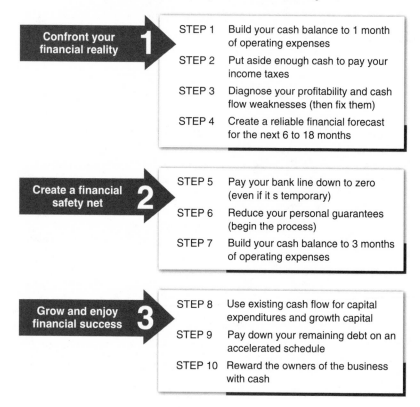

It's a simple system you can implement in baby steps. It's a system that will help you move toward financial health, wealth, and freedom. (Yes, freedom. One of the reasons to improve your profitability and cash flow is to give you the freedom to run your business in a way that fits with your lifestyle and your goals in life.)

It will provide you with the clarity of knowing what your next steps are. That way you can shift your focus to specific action plans and away from the fuzziness that too often creates struggle and confusion in business.

PART 1: CONFRONT YOUR FINANCIAL REALITY

This part of the three-part plan is about assessing, then improving, the financial health of your business. Confronting the reality of your financial situation is a vital first step.

It's similar to the approach you would take if you were not feeling well physically. If you didn't feel well for an extended period of time, you would eventually decide to go see the doctor. You would want to find out what's wrong and find out what you need to do to start feeling better. The doctor would ask a number of questions about your symptoms. He or she would take your blood pressure and possibly take blood (ouch). The doctor is making an assessment of what kind of problem you have and how serious it might be. A treatment plan cannot be made until the problem is properly diagnosed.

The process is similar when it comes to improving the financial health of your business. We first look at the symptoms. Then we work on the diagnosis and treatment plan.

> "Have you ever worked for an unprofitable business? If you have, you probably learned that it's not much fun. Perhaps people who work at unprofitable businesses should consider putting signs in their offices that say, 'It ain't fun if it ain't profitable.'
>
> If you have worked for both profitable and unprofitable businesses, we think you would agree it's more fun when the enterprise is actually making money. We have never heard anybody complain about excessive frugality in successful businesses; but we sure have heard about 'the need to tighten up' in an unprofitable one."
>
> —Lawrence L. Steinmetz, PhD., and William T. Brooks,
> *How to Sell at Margins Higher Than Your Competitors*

I break the process down into four steps. These four steps are a unique combination of small steps (baby steps) that will help you quickly assess your financial health. You will be surprised how fast you begin to hone in on the solution once you clear away the fog that is clouding your vision.

Here are the four steps.

Step 1: Build your cash balance to one month of expenses

If you have less than one month of operating expenses in the bank, you are probably experiencing unnecessary stress, angering your vendors, irritating your employees, ignoring the financial reality of your business, and generally making your life harder than it needs to be. Maintaining a very small bank balance in business turns otherwise simple decisions and processes into complicated and time-consuming hassles.

To implement step 1, you first need to determine the number that approximates one month of operating expenses. I exclude cost of goods sold (unless you have employee expenses or other operating type expenses in cost of goods sold). With that number defined, you can determine whether you already have one month of operating expenses in the bank. If you do, then check step 1 as complete.

If you are short of the one-month target, then put a dollar amount on how much cash you need to "find." Let's say your monthly operating expenses are in the $1,000,000 range and your bank balance has been hovering around $750,000. So your goal in this example is to add $250,000 to your cash balance.

Now you have to ask yourself two thought-provoking questions (in this order):

1. How *fast* can I come up with an extra $250,000?
2. *Where* is the $250,000 going to come from?

I love these two questions because they generate fascinating reactions and thoughts in your mind. The first question forces you to consider just how long it might take you to achieve your goal. One month? Two months? Twelve months? The second question puts your focus on where you're going to generate the cash from. Sometimes the goal looks easy and the answer is obvious. Other times it creates dread and fear.

Either way, there's no need to solve the problem just yet. Just spend a little time thinking about how you are going to build your cash balance. Then on to step 2.

[NOTE: If you have a bank line of credit, and use your cash to pay down the line daily, it's OK to move directly to step 2. You will dig deeper into how you are using the line (and your availability under the line) in steps 3, 4, and 5.]

Step 2: Put aside enough cash to pay your income taxes

Taxes should be set aside during the year, not at the end of the year. The government yields way too big a stick to make a mistake when it comes to paying your income taxes. This is one of those "unforced errors" that plagues smaller businesses more so than larger ones. Income tax payments should never be a surprise.

To implement step 2, you need to:

- Estimate your income tax expense for the year.
- Look at how much cash you have already put aside for income taxes.
- Determine the amount of cash, if any, that still needs to be put aside.

Let's say it's November and your tax year ends in December. You estimate that your taxable income for the year will be $1,000,000.

Using 40% as an estimate of the tax rate, your tax expense is estimated at $400,000. What you have put aside already (in this case through estimated tax payments) is $325,000.

That means you have $75,000 of cash that needs to be set aside so you have a total of $400,000 put away for income taxes.

Step 3: Diagnose your profitability and cash flow weaknesses (then fix them)

Financial struggle in business has its roots in profitability challenges and/or the way in which you monitor and manage your cash flow. The secret to keeping this step simple is to think strategically and high level about your financial performance before you begin diving into the details. Why? Because there is probably more work involved in this step than any other step in the process.

It is very easy to get lost in the weeds as you work to diagnose (then fix) your profitability and cash weaknesses. For example, when you begin assessing your profitability, you will have lots of questions run through your mind. Questions like:

- Could I be more profitable?
- By how much?
- Says who?
- Based on what?
- Do I have a revenue problem?
- Do I have an expense problem?
- Should I raise my prices?

The way you combat the problem of getting lost in the weeds is to begin by looking at the big picture first. Let's go up and get the 30,000-foot view of how your business is performing financially. That approach will help you create some interesting insights that will guide you on the path to a clearer view of your current financial reality.

The work in this step is broken up into three components.

Understand and articulate the three largest drivers of cash for the last six months (in a 2-minute conversation). The first thing you do is "follow the money." You do that by answering one question: "What happened to the cash?" Specifically, you want to answer that question for the last six-month period. I like to answer this question using the Cash Flow Focus Report. It is a super-fast way to highlight the three largest drivers of cash, provide a one-line description for each driver (for each of the large changes in cash), and decide whether each change is good or bad. You can learn more about the Cash Flow Focus Report at www.ILoveForecasting.com.

Create the 5-Minute Profitability Assessment (to determine what your profitability should be). The purpose of this analysis is to quickly determine if your business is as profitable as it should be.

For example, in one company the owner was frustrated because cash was always tight despite the fact that they had made big strides in becoming profitable over the last two years. After completing the analysis, it turns out that profits were only 4% of sales in a business where the norm is closer to 10%. At $4,000,000 in revenues, that meant their Profitability Gap was $240,000 (10% – 4% × $4,000,000). Now that they had put a number on the profit improvement target (the opportunity), the mission became "closing the profitability gap."

The goal of this 5-minute assessment is to come up with an estimate of what your annual profit should be (or could be). Your estimate doesn't have to be *right*. It just needs to be a number you can write down. You will have plenty of time later to explore your estimate in more detail to determine if it should become your new profitability target.

Here's the exercise. Take 5 minutes to come up with an estimate of how much money you should make each year in your business. Here are the steps:

- Look at your pre-tax income (your profit before income taxes) for the last twelve months. Divide that number by your revenues (total sales). Jot that percentage down. Let's say that revenues are $10,000,000 and pre-tax profit is $500,000. So the percentage is 5%.
- Look at your gross margin (gross profit dollars divided by revenues). Use that percentage to lookup your pre-tax profit target range in Figure B1-2. Let's say gross profit is $4,200,000. So

Figure B1-2
PRE-TAX PROFIT TARGET RANGE

Gross Margin	Pre-Tax Profit Target Range
5% to 25%	1% to 10% of revenues
25% to 40%	10% to 15% of revenues
40% and above	15% to 20% of revenues

the gross margin is 42%. The pre-tax profit range in the table would be 15% to 20% of revenues.

- Choose a pre-tax profit percentage in the range and multiply that times revenues. Write that number down. In my example, I'll choose 15% (to be conservative). That number times $10,000,000 in revenues is a pre-tax profit target of $1,500,000.

In my example the profit target is $1,500,000 and the actual profit is $500,000. The Profitability Gap is the difference, or $1,000,000. Remember, it's just an estimate . . . for now. You will have time to more fully analyze that number later.

> "When it comes to pretax profit, here's what I've found to be true for the vast majority of businesses:
> - 5 percent or less of pretax profit means your business is on life support.
> - 10 percent of pretax profit means you have a good business.
> - 15 percent or more of pretax profit means you have a great business."
>
> —Greg Crabtree, *Simple Numbers, Straight Talk, Big Profits!*

Discover where cash is being "trapped" in the business. The primary focus here is on inventory, accounts receivable, and accounts payable. These "working capital" related accounts oftentimes hide opportunities and problems (and cash) because most entrepreneurs pay little attention to them month-to-month.

I like to measure the days of inventory outstanding (DIO) when evaluating inventory levels, days of sales outstanding (DSO) when evaluating accounts receivable balances, and days of payables (DPO) when evaluating accounts payable. I evaluate the trend to see if it looks like there might be some cash hiding in there (or problems hiding in accounts payable).

You would be surprised how paying closer attention to these accounts, and the metrics that drive the balances, can highlight sloppiness that can be fixed quickly. And "fixing" the problem produces instant cash!

Step 4: Create a reliable financial forecast for the next six to eighteen months

By *reliable*, I mean the forecast is a tool for strategic decision making. It is a tool for making *better* business decisions. By *forecast*, I'm referring to a fully modeled set of financial statements including the income statement, balance sheet, and statement of cash flows in the same format you use for monthly financial reporting.

**One of the most powerful tools in business
is a reliable financial forecast.**

A reliable financial forecast is meant to help you:

- Define where your business is going financially (and where you want it to go).
- Shine a light on the dangers and opportunities that lie ahead of you on your journey.
- Create a roadmap to get you there safely and on time.
- Monitor your pace and progress on your journey to success.

It's a tool for hooking your vision and strategy for the business up to the likely financial implications of achieving your plan. It's your view through the financial windshield of your business.

When you know where you are going and you have a plan to get you there safely and on time, you will feel a sense of courage, confidence, and peace of mind. This is why financial forecasting is such a powerful tool in business. In essence, it forces you to think strategically about your business and where you want your business to go. It encourages you to paint a picture of what business and financial success look like in a way that is revealing and enlightening.

You will be pleasantly surprised by the confidence and courage you feel once you have a reliable financial forecast at work in your business.

PART 2: CREATE A FINANCIAL SAFETY NET

Wikipedia says a safety net is "a net to protect people from injury after falling from heights by limiting the distance they fall, and deflecting to dissipate the impact energy." A safety net helps the circus performer on the high wire avoid death (and protects the audience from watching them splat on the ground) if they make a mistake during a performance.

The safety net also frees the performer up to take more chances. They can learn more difficult and advanced "moves" knowing they are protected from the inevitable falls that come with learning and experimenting. That way they can put on an amazing performance for their audience.

In business, a financial safety net is created by having some money (cash in the bank) and less debt.

And it provides you the same two benefits: it protects you when financial surprises hit (avoiding the splat on the ground) and it allows you to take measured risks (learning and experimenting) to grow your company.

A financial surprise could be a sudden reduction in sales, a large customer that pays late, or an unexpected expense that blows a hole in your budget. Without a safety net, you have to scramble to avoid disaster or embarrassment with vendors or employees. With a safety net, you simply deal with the surprise and move on. No drama. No losing sleep.

Taking a measured risk could be hiring that new sales manager you think can double sales. The risk is the new sales manager might not land any new sales. You might lose money because you are paying them a base salary to get started. It could be a total flop. Without a safety net, you might have to reduce other expenses to make up for the shortfall. Or you might have to borrow money just to get by. With a safety net, you know in advance that if the worst case happens you can live with it. You can write the check and move on. No drama. No losing sleep.

Step 5: Pay your bank line down to zero (even if temporary)

A revolving line of credit is meant to, well, *revolve.* You borrow on the line in order to meet seasonal demands or address other short-term cash needs. Then the bank line should be paid back down to zero.

A good example of a revolving line of credit is a company that carries inventory and whose sales are highly seasonal. Ahead of the busy selling season it has to increase inventory levels. The bank line can be drawn on to fund the inventory purchases. As the seasonal selling comes to a close, and the increase in inventory has been sold and converted to cash, the company can pay down the line. It had a temporary need to borrow money and the bank line gave the company the flexibility to meet its cash needs.

The problem is that many businesses borrow on their bank line for other than temporary cash needs. Sometimes it's used for capital expenditures. Sometimes to fund losses. Sometimes to fund owner distributions. The availability of cash from the line can easily lead to decisions that have serious consequences later. The discipline of forcing yourself to pay off your bank line at least once a year (or more) will help ensure you are using the bank line the way it was intended.

Step 6: Reduce your personal guarantees (begin the process)

In the early days of building a business it can be difficult to avoid personal guarantees. But as you grow and become more successful, you have more leverage, and more reason, to purposefully begin reducing your personal guarantees. Most businesses are run inside a legal entity like a corporation or limited liability company (LLC) in order to provide some liability protection for its owners. Legal entities have assets and liabilities separate and apart from those who own the entities.

A personal guarantee is you agreeing to take personal responsibility as an owner for a specific debt or obligation of the business. So if the company files bankruptcy, or fails to pay the obligation, you are personally responsible to make the payment.

Most entrepreneurs and business owners rarely consider how much they have personally guaranteed. And they are shocked at the total dollar amount they are personally responsible for. One reason the number is so surprising, and so big, is because the guarantees have occurred over a number of years as the business has grown. You finance some new equipment and the loan requires you to sign a personal guarantee. You sign a new lease or renew an agreement with an important supplier and a personal guarantee is part of the deal. Over time, as your business grows, the number and amount of obligations you've guaranteed goes up.

But as you grow your business and become more successful, it's wise to think more strategically and thoughtfully about how you handle personal guarantees. You do that in two ways. First, quantify the amount of your existing guarantees.

Figure B1-3 is a format to help you list and quantify your existing personal guarantees.

Figure B1-3
YOUR PERSONAL GUARANTEES

Obligations I Have Personally Guaranteed	
Bank or lender debt I have guaranteed	$ _____
Lease or related obligations I have guaranteed	$ _____
Supply agreements/obligations I have guaranteed	$ _____
Vendor contracts/obligations I have guaranteed	$ _____
Franchise agreements/obligations I have guaranteed	$ _____
Other commitments/obligations I have guaranteed	$ _____
Total amount I have personally guaranteed	$ _____

Second, slowly begin reducing the number of guarantees. One of the best places to start is to refuse to sign any new vendor or supplier guarantees. Most vendors put the guarantee on their credit form but that doesn't mean you have to sign it. They will almost always set up credit with the business as the only responsible party.

Step 7: Build your cash balance to three months of operating expenses

Building your bank balance to three months of operating expenses creates a cash cushion against surprises. And it provides "dry powder" so you can quickly jump on unique business opportunities that might come your way. Not to mention the fact that there's nothing like a healthy cash balance to help you sleep well at night.

PART 3: GROW AND ENJOY FINANCIAL SUCCESS

Growing a successful business is much harder than most people realize. Only a small number of people have the unique talents and drive to build and manage a company through the many ups and downs inherent in business. Even fewer people can grow while at the same time making the company worth more and more money along the way.

Ultimately, your financial goal in business is to create wealth and freedom.

I like to define wealth as having a strong net worth (assets greater than your liabilities – both in the business and personally). For one person, that might be a $1,000,000 net worth. To another person that might be a $25,000,000 net worth. Or put another way, having a strong net worth is about "having money." Money helps make a lot of things in life just a little bit easier. It gives you options. It makes it easier to help other people by sharing a portion of the financial resources you have accumulated.

Of course, money isn't necessarily the only prize in business. There is the pride of accomplishing something very challenging. There is the knowledge that you helped your customers and team members along the way. There is the freedom and peace of mind that comes from taking a risk and winning.

These last three steps in the process help you set the stage for a future that is even bigger and brighter than your past.

Step 8: Use existing cash flow for capital expenditures and growth capital

Capital expenditures generally take two forms. The first I refer to as "maintenance capital expenditures." These are expenditures, or investments, that maintain your existing fixed asset base. Generally speaking, they help prevent decline. The second is "growth-related capital expenditures." These are meant to add new income-producing assets. They are designed to add to your ability to serve more customers, drive revenues higher, and increase profitability and cash flow. You are wise to fund both with internally generated cash as you grow and become stronger financially.

Step 9: Pay down your remaining debt on an accelerated schedule

Debt can be an important tool in helping you build your business. But with financial success comes the ability to pay your debt down on an accelerated schedule. Use a portion of your existing cash flow and allocate it to a more aggressive payment plan. It will feel weird at first. But you will come to love the feeling of strength and accomplishment watching your debt levels shrink.

Step 10: Reward the owners of the business with cash

The ultimate financial reward for a business owner is receiving healthy distributions of the company's excess cash. It's your reward as an investor. It's your reward for building a successful company. It's cash you can invest in other assets or ventures as part of building a sizable net worth for you and your family. It's a fantastic way to enjoy the fruits of financial success.

START SLOW

When you have a step-by-step plan to follow you'll find that managing your business gets easier. Start slow. No need to speed through the three-part plan. I designed it so you can implement it in small steps. One foot in front of the other.

Start by implementing step 1. You will begin to see progress much faster than you might imagine. Then you can begin thinking through each of the other steps in the process.

Bonus Chapter 2

How to Turn Your Accounting Department into a Strategic Asset

"The fact is, accounting and finance, like all those other business disciplines, really are as much art as they are science. You might call this the CFO's or the controller's hidden secret, except that it isn't really a secret, it's a widely acknowledged truth that everyone in finance knows."

—Karen Berman and Joe Knight with John Case,
Financial Intelligence

What if you could turn the accounting and financial function within your business into an important strategic asset? An asset that could help you win in business? An asset that could help you create confidence and credibility with all the people interested in, and invested in, the financial success of your company?

A poor accounting and financial function will drag you down. It handcuffs your ability to grow and attract capital and talent. It hurts your credibility with your banker, lenders, investors, partners, and all those in the financial community you need to grow your business successfully. It will suck the life out of you. What a waste of smarts and talent to work so hard to create a successful company only to allow your accounting function to underperform and drag you down.

In this bonus chapter, I'm going to help you evaluate your accounting and finance function, what some consider a necessary evil, and turn it into an asset the financial community respects and admires and that forms the foundation for helping you grow and succeed financially. This isn't about winning awards in accounting. This is 100% focused on making your business stronger.

Smart Financial Management

Smart management in business starts with taking a more strategic approach to how you manage the financial side of your business. You have a unique opportunity to build confidence, trust, and credibility with everyone who has a stake in the financial success of the company. Smart financial management is made up of three components:

- Confidence
- Insight
- Accuracy and speed

These three components of smart financial management are your guide to turning your accounting function into a strategic asset. You can transform their role into one of helping you create trust and respect and away from the old view of accounting as just gatekeepers and a cost center.

Confidence

The foundation for success in managing the financial side of the business is captured in this one word–confidence. Confidence in your own mind that your company has a solid financial foundation in place to grow. Confidence in the minds of the bankers, lenders, investors, and shareholders who will provide the capital you need to improve and expand your business. Confidence that you and your management team have fast, accurate, and focused financial information to make smart business decisions.

Insight

The information you receive about the financial side of your business needs to be insightful. Too many entrepreneurs (even CFOs) fall short here because they see their role as just requiring (or preparing) financial statements . . . or a tax return . . . or creating an analysis schedule.

Providing insight goes way past that. It's about providing information that helps management make better decisions. It's about providing information to lenders and investors to help them better understand the key drivers of your financial performance. Financial information that is insightful is an important part of creating confidence and trust in their eyes.

Accuracy and Speed

The third component of smart financial management has to do with the accuracy and speed with which you receive (and provide) financial information. Providing slow and inaccurate information will kill your credibility. No one will trust your numbers if you do that. Nothing kills your credibility more than providing financial information that is inaccurate or tends to bounce around and change.

When you provide accurate information, and you provide it quickly after the end of the month, and you do that consistently month to month, you set yourself out as a company that has its act together. Lenders and investors love that and it will help you forge a strong relationship with them that will last a long, long time. . . and pay big dividends.

Financial Team Assessment

Now I'll weave the three characteristics of smart financial management into an assessment form so you can quickly see where you stand in each area. It's a tool to help you better visualize what your financial function should look like while also providing a hard look at where you are today. By financial function, or financial team, I am referring to your accounting department and the related departments responsible for the financial side of your business. Basically, the area your CFO manages.

The Financial Team Assessment in Figure B2-1 is a super-fast way for you to zero in on where you are weak or strong. You can quickly see where you stand in the three areas that matter most. The three components of the assessment tie in directly to the three keys to smart financial management we just looked at. Your score in each of those three areas provides an instant picture about the health and well-being of your accounting and finance function.

Here's How the Assessment Works

Each section has a number of statements in it. Read each statement and then answer, on a scale of 1 to 10, the extent to which that statement is true in your company. Write your answer in the blank to the left of each statement. A 10 means "absolutely, 100% true." A 1 means "not true at all, not even close."

For example, the first statement in the Confidence Factor section says "Your accounting and finance function is strong and will support your growth plans into the future." So how true is that statement in your company? If your accounting and finance function operates as a well-oiled machine, you would answer with a 9 or a 10. If it's pretty strong, but there are some areas where you would like to see it get better, the answer might be an 8. If it has some things under control but you know you have to make it stronger in order to help

Figure B2-1
FINANCIAL TEAM ASSESSMENT

The three sections below provide a quick way for you to gauge how effective your accounting and financial function is currently performing. Answer each statement on a scale of 1 to 10 as to how true that statement is. A 1 means "not true at all, not even close" and a 10 means "absolutely, 100% true".

	CONFIDENCE FACTOR
	Your accounting and finance function is strong and will support your growth plans into the future
	Your bank/lenders have confidence in your numbers and the financials they receive
	Your Board/owners have confidence in your numbers and the financials they receive
	Your management team has confidence in the numbers and the financials they receive
	Add up each of the answers
	Divide by number of questions answered
	= Your Confidence Factor Score

	INSIGHT FACTOR
	You provide a monthly reporting package to lenders and owners
	The package contains:
	A short memo that answers the question "What happened and what's about to happen"
	Actual results for the 5 to 7 key drivers of financial performance
	Current month and year-to-date results vs plan and prior year
	Insight into "What happened to the cash and what's about to happen to the cash?"
	Side-by-side view of actual and forecast monthly results down to the cash flow level
	Add up each of the answers
	Divide by number of questions answered
	= Your Insight Factor Score

	ACCURACY AND SPEED FACTOR
	The numbers in the monthly financial statements are accurate
	Financial statements are prepared in accordance with Generally Accepted Accounting Principles (GAAP)
	In the annual review or audit of your financial statements, the CPA firm makes very few adjustments
	Each account on the balance sheet is well supported and documented
	Management reviews the monthly financial statements to ensure accuracy before they are published
	Financial statements are provided to lenders and owners on or before the 10th calendar day each month
	Add up each of the answers
	Divide by number of questions answered
	= Your Accuracy and Speed Factor Score

you grow the company into the future, you might answer with a 6 or a 7. If the function is in shambles you might answer anywhere from a 1 to a 5.

The key is to go with your gut reaction to each statement. No need to think too much about your answer or be overly precise. You just want to get a quick sense of where you stand on each statement. Then each of the three sections has a space for you to add up your answers, divide by the number of questions you answered, and the result is your score on that factor. The score should have one decimal place. It's a very simple process, yet very revealing.

Let's talk about each factor in a little more detail.

Confidence Factor

This score is what it's all about. This is how you know if your accounting and finance function is strong and helping you win friends and influence people (the people who provide access to cash) or if it is weak and dragging you down. It helps you determine whether this part of your business is an exciting contributor to your success, or just a cost center that fails to add any real value.

There are only four statements to respond to.

1. **Your accounting and finance function is strong and will support your growth plans into the future**

   Go with your gut reaction to answer this question. What was your first thought when you read that statement? One part of your reaction hinged on the word "strong." The other part of your reaction was to the words "will support your growth plans into the future." The faster you want to grow, and the larger you want to become, the stronger your foundation has to be. . . and the better your financial information and reporting has to be. And growth requires cash from both internal and external sources. Growing successfully means you have a good view of

182

what lies ahead financially and that you can line up cash *before* you need it. A weak accounting and finance function provides poor visibility and does little to help you create trust and respect in the financial community.

2. **Your bank/lenders have confidence in your numbers and the financials they receive**

   Anyone you have borrowed money from fits here. Do they have confidence in the financial statements you provide? Do they trust your numbers? The more sophisticated the lenders, the more likely they are to analyze the financials you provide and use them as an important tool in evaluating your company (and you) as an ongoing credit. Most companies do a poor job in this area. A 10 here means lenders frequently praise you for the quality and speed with which you provide them good, solid financials they can trust. Complaints and lots of questions about the numbers puts you in the 1–5 range.

3. **Your investors/shareholders have confidence in your numbers and the financials they receive**

   This is the same question as 2 but focused on your investors/ shareholders and owners. The larger your company, the more likely you have owners in addition to yourself (and a Board of Directors). And they have a unique view of the company that is very important to think through and understand. They are usually not involved in the day-to-day functioning of the company. But they have a great deal of responsibility and a vested interest in the financial success of the company. So they need to get information in a way that helps them play that role and helps them understand the financials from the 30,000-foot view. They must understand the basic drivers of financial success without needing to dive into the details of the day-to-day operations. The more confidence they have in the financial information they receive from you, the more support and back-ing they will provide you and your company.

4. **Your management team has confidence in the numbers and the financials they receive**

   This is the same question as 2 and 3, but focused on your man-agement team. Management needs financial reporting that helps them instantly see the link between the actions they are taking and the financial results those actions created (or are likely to create). They need to know quickly what they should be doing more of (because it is creating the desired financial result) and what they need to do different (because it is not creating the desired financial result). That's how the accounting and finance function can add tremendous value in your ongo-ing effort to improve profitability and increase cash flow.

What's the Norm?

My experience with clients is that most Confidence Factor Scores will be in 7.5 to 8.5 range. Generally, the financial statements are in pretty good shape and the parties receiving them are generally okay with them. The area bringing the score down is usually that the owner or entrepreneur knows in his gut that the function is a weak link in the organization.

They have plans for growing the company much bigger than it is and they are beginning to realize that having a strong and respected financial function will help them make that happen. And they also realize that the function will be an anchor around their neck if they neglect it. They looked at that function purely as a cost center in the past and allowed it to lag behind the rest of the organization.

Now they are beginning to see that growing the company and improving in a substantial way requires a solid foundation built on strong accounting. They have come to realize that it is smart management to think of that function more strategically than they have in the past. They have decided to turn what some consider a necessary evil into a strength that makes the journey ahead much more likely to be a financially successful and rewarding one.

The other area that brings the score down is a lender that is unhappy on some level. In one company, the lender was somewhat irritated by the slow reporting the company provided each month but they were not kicking and screaming. The bigger problem was management could not provide insight into *why* the numbers were what they were. Working capital had been changing meaningfully during the year and the bank could never get an insightful answer as to why. So they were losing confidence not so much in the financial statements, but in management's lack of understanding of the changes happening in the numbers. And it is difficult to have a Confidence Factor score in the 9 to 10 range when you have a banker or a lender whose confidence in you is waning.

Generally speaking, the goal is to be between a 9 and a 10. A score between 7 and 9 means there is work to do. A score less than 7 means you have a big problem on your hands and you need to get about fixing it fast.

Insight Factor

The Insight Factor score is focused on the quality and insightfulness of your existing financial reporting process. It is a subtle but very important quality that helps instill confidence in the minds of lenders, investors, your board, and anyone else you share financial information with. This is where thinking strategically pays big dividends. Why just plop a package of financial information on these very important people when you can provide the information in a way that is thoughtful and helps instill confidence in their minds. That confidence becomes an asset that will help you achieve your growth objectives. It also enhances your credibility and helps you stand out as a company that has its act together.

What's missing in your current financial reporting process, and it creates an exciting opportunity for you, is it lacks *insight*. It misses a golden opportunity to use the monthly reporting package as a killer tool to instill confidence and credibility in the minds of the people receiving it.

Here's how that gets started in most companies. The bank or another lender wants financial statements. So you say, "Okay, they want financial statements – let's give them the financials." Sounds logical. The mindset starts with basically giving them what they asked for.

The opportunity though is in looking at their request from a more strategic perspective. You want to jump on their request for financial information by saying, "Excellent, we have an opportunity now to foster a unique relationship here. What a perfect time to plant the seeds of credibility and trust with these guys." When you do that your mind shifts into how to provide insightful information that helps you stand head and shoulders above their other customers.

So you provide summary information on the key drivers of financial performance in addition to just the financial statements. You provide comparisons to plan and prior year. You provide information in a side-by-side format so trends and direction jump off the page at them. You provide a forecast so they have a view of where you are going financially. You serve up valuable information for them on a silver platter. That's how you drive confidence and trust with lenders and investors.

And one thing you should know about lenders. Most lenders take the basic financial statements you provide and load them into some sort of financial analysis tool in order to make them more insightful. That requires work and time. When you provide a more insightful package to them they get even better information without having to do the extra work. *That gets their attention.* You stand out as a smarter company than the other customers they deal with every day.

Here are the six statements in this section of the assessment.

1. **You provide a monthly reporting package to lenders and owners**

   This statement is similar to the strategy in selling where sometimes you have to "Go for the no." In selling, especially in big-ticket items with a long selling cycle, some people believe you have to ask some questions and if you get a "no" then the prospect is not qualified and you don't end up wasting tons of selling time with them. (Not everyone believes in that advice but I have seen it work very effectively in certain businesses.)

   If you don't currently provide a monthly financial reporting package of some sort to lenders and owners then you can answer this with a zero (meaning NO). Then the other statements in this section get a zero as well and your Insight Factor score is, you guessed it, zero.

   If you provide a financial reporting package each month that you consider to be very useful, then your answer would be a 10. If you provide a package but it is not monthly or you know it needs to be better and more useful and relevant for the user, then just use your gut to provide your rating.

   The next five statements relate to what is included in your monthly reporting package. They are all preceded by the words "The package contains." I have included that part of the statement so it is easier to see what each statement is referring to in your existing reporting package.

2. **The package contains: A short memo that answers the question "What happened and what's about to happen?"**

   A one- or two-page memo is a powerful way to simplify and summarize your financial results for the month. Do you provide one in your monthly reporting package? Picture in your mind each person that will be receiving this package. Imagine they receive the package and before they look at it they are asking themselves this question "I wonder how the month turned out? And I wonder where their results are headed?" The job of your monthly reporting package is to very quickly answer those questions for them. If they get to the answers quickly, then the package has done its job. If they have to dig and ask a bunch of follow-up questions, then it has failed to do its job. A one- or two-page memo is a fantastic tool.

3. **The package contains: Actual results for the 5 to 7 key drivers of financial performance**

   The typical financial reporting package just provides the basic financial statements (although many tend to leave out the cash flow statement, which is a big mistake). You provide real insight for the user, though, when you help them see and understand the handful of key drivers of financial performance. It promotes a deeper understanding of your business. It makes them smarter about how your business generates results. It helps them to more easily understand the parts of the business that have the most impact on your financial performance.

4. **The package contains: Current month and year-to-date results vs. plan and prior year**

   It is important to look at results for the year compared to both plan and the same period of the prior year. That raises a big question: Do you make it easy for the user to see how revenues, margins, expenses, and profitability compare to the plan and how they compare to last year? The comparisons don't have to be on the same page, but there needs to be a presentation in the package that gives the user a chance to see how actual results compare to the plan and how results compare to the same period in the prior year.

5. **The package contains: Insight into "What happened to the cash and what's about to happen to the cash?"**

   Ultimately your success in business is going to be determined by the degree to which you create and hang on to cash. Everything ultimately comes down to cash and cash flow. Cash is what pays the bills. Cash is what pays down the debt. Cash is what's required in order to invest and grow your company. Cash is ultimately what is going to help you and your family retire in style and comfort. But understanding and managing cash flow is not a straightforward process. Especially when you are trying to help investors and lenders understand what's going on with your company's cash flow. You have to take information from the financial statements, distill it down, and present it in a way that the financial statements, by themselves, do a poor job of. You want the reader of your financial reporting package to instantly understand what happened to the cash. And you want to do it in a way that highlights the key drivers of cash flow. People tend to think only in terms of profitability. But profitability and cash flow are not the same. You need visibility in terms of what happened to the cash, and what's about to happen to the cash.

6. **The package contains: Side-by-side view of actual and forecast monthly results down to the cash flow level**

   Something magical happens when a person sees monthly financial results side-by-side. Seeing actual results side-by-side, together with forecast results, provides amazing clarity. It instantly provides insight into trends and whether the numbers make sense or not. Very few companies provide this kind of unique and transparent view into their financial results. And I'm not just talking about the income statement here. I also mean the balance sheet is presented with each month side-by-side. And the same thing for cash flow. This may be the fastest way to create respect with the financial community (absent just sending them a big check for no reason)! Virtually no one is doing this for them, which makes it even easier, and makes it more powerful and impactful, when you serve it up for them on a silver platter.

What's the Norm?

My experience with clients is that most Insight Factor scores will be in the 5 to 6 range. Remember, the goal here is to be at a 9 to 10. That's a *big* gap. The reason the gap is not even wider is that most companies growing through the $20 million to $50 million revenue range have already started providing some form of financial information to the outside world – usually for the bank or lender or other investors they brought in along the way. So the fact that you are providing a financial package of some sort helps keep the score from going too much below 5.

The issue comes in because most companies miss the opportunity to turn the monthly reporting process into something more strategic. You want to use the monthly reporting process to enhance your credibility, influence, and trust with that audience. Make it super simple for them to understand the key drivers of your results. Provide comparisons of actual vs. plan so they can quickly see what's working and not working. Highlight the key drivers of cash for the month so they can see how you are managing all the different drivers of cash flow.

Provide them a view through the financial windshield of your business so they know not only what happened in the past but what's about to happen in the future. Take the opportunity to serve it up to them on a silver platter. That's how you drive confidence and trust with lenders and investors.

Accuracy and Speed Factor

This score could also be called the Trust Factor score. It is a great predictor of how well the users of your financials trust the information you provide. Trust is a huge part of your goal of creating confidence and credibility with those who are invested in one form or another in your financial success.

Consider this thought for a minute. Let's say someone asked you to invest some money in an idea they had. You like the person and you really want to help them. But you had this nagging voice in your head saying "I'm not really sure I trust what he is telling me. There's some inconsistencies here that I'm not sure I'm comfortable with."

If your brain is sending you signals that question whether you can really trust the information you are getting, it is going to make you unsure and uncomfortable all over. And that is *not* a recipe for saying "Yes."

Same way in your company.

You dramatically increase your odds of success when you purposefully and strategically plant seeds of trust with everyone interested in, and invested in, your financial success.

This is especially true for those people who are partners with you in providing the cash and the financial backing to help you and your company grow and succeed.

Here are the six statements in this section of the assessment.

1. **The numbers in the monthly financial statements are accurate**

   This sounds like a no-brainer. But it's not. There are a lot of businesses, especially those closely held, where this is a real problem. This speaks to the quality of the accounting processes and controls used to gather, record, and report transactions in your accounting system. That process has to be solid and very tightly managed. Bad numbers will kill your credibility with lenders and investors. And bad numbers will cause your management team to make bad decisions. Kind of like giving your doctor inaccurate information about an ailment you have and wondering why the diagnosis (and treatment) come back wrong. Or driving along, following the directions on your GPS, only to find out the wrong address had been entered in the GPS. The directions you are following are taking you to a place you don't want to go.

2. **Financial statements are prepared in accordance with Generally Accepted Accounting Principles (GAAP)**

   This point goes past whether your numbers are accurate. The question here is whether your financial statements are prepared in accordance with GAAP. This is one of the larger mistakes companies make when providing financial statements outside the company. Owners tend to provide monthly or quarterly financial statements to lenders and investors and let their CPA firm "adjust" the financials when they come in to do their annual review or audit. That's a big mistake. It undermines your credibility. The financial community concludes you are not professional enough to provide GAAP financials each month. Remember, they are experienced financial people. They know what they want. And they expect you to be sharp enough to provide them GAAP financials.

3. **In the annual review or audit of your financial statements, the CPA firm makes very few adjustments**

   When your CPA firm does their year-end work and they have to make lots of adjustments to your financial statements, what they are doing is *fixing your mistakes*. This is either because transactions were recorded improperly or because transactions were not recorded at all. Basically, when points #1 and #2 are a problem, the CPA firm has to do the work for you so they have good financial statements to work with. And that means the financial statements you have been using to manage the business all year, and providing to lenders and investors all year, have been *wrong*. Your goal is to provide accurate and complete financial statements every month. That means there should be no need for the CPA firm to come in and "adjust" your financial statements. Why? Because you did them right the first time. And you won't have to experience the embarrassment of having to tell everyone that the financial statements you provided them were wrong (and explain to them what the CPA firm had to fix for you).

4. **Each account on the balance sheet is well supported and documented**

Are the various amounts on your balance sheet well supported? Do you know what makes up those balances? The reason you want a super clean balance sheet is because that is where nasty financial surprises tend to hide. You seldom walk into a really nice home only to find a dirty, messy, disorganized interior once you walk in. Here's a little secret that few owners truly understand. Financial statements prepared in accordance with GAAP are full of estimates. And the balance sheet is where many of those estimates reside (and accumulate). It requires the time and attention of someone who understands financial statements to ensure those estimates don't accumulate (and eventually rot and die). The accounts on the balance sheet need to be monitored, evaluated, and documented every month to make sure they are as accurate as possible.

5. **Management reviews the monthly financial statements to ensure accuracy before they are published**

It's important for management to do a detailed review of the financial statements every month. You want to understand what's in there. You want to be in tune with how the results compare to plan and how they compare to what you were expecting for the month. You want to ask questions. Why is this number so high? I was expecting that number to be different. You don't want to fly at the 30,000-foot level and just assume that everything is okay. It's going to help you later when one of your lenders or investors has a question and they ask you about it. You should be able to answer most questions they have very quickly because you know what's going on relative to the plan and relative to what you expected the financial results to be.

6. **Financial statements are provided to lenders and investors on or before the 10th calendar day each month**

   An important part of creating trust and credibility with the users of your financial statements is to provide your reporting package promptly and predictably every month. I don't get too hung up on whether it's the 10th calendar day or the 15th calendar day. We're not trying to create any awards for the fastest financial closing process (neither of those dates would accomplish that). The key is to choose the date and provide the statements on or before that date religiously every month. That way lenders and investors/owners always know when to expect your financial reporting package. It demonstrates discipline and predictability in the way you run the financial side of the business. It helps build confidence and trust. It helps you stand out in their minds as different (and better) than many of the companies they deal with. And that is an important part of your goal here.

What's the Norm?

My experience with clients is that most Accuracy and Speed Factor scores will be in the 5 to 8 range. What generally drives their score down is an overreliance on the outside CPA firm to make year-end adjustments to the financial statements. When you do that, you are publishing monthly financial statements that are incomplete and inaccurate. Sometimes it's leaving depreciation and amortization entries for the CPA firm. Or saving decisions on which expenditures must be capitalized to the end of the year. Or applying debt service payments to principal, and then having the CPA firm record the allocation between interest and principal. And a range of other examples where you leave the "accounting details" to the CPA firm after the year is over. This is a common practice in smaller companies and one you need to fix as you mature as a company and attempt to create credibility and trust with lenders and investors.

Another area that drives scores down is not paying close attention to the balance sheet. Most of the focus from management is generally on the income statement. So the balance sheet does not get much attention – sometimes even from the accountants. It's a huge blind spot for many companies because managing cash flow, and managing profitability, requires that you know exactly what's going on in each of the balance line items. Ignoring inventory, receivables, capital expenditures, payables, and a host of other balance sheet accounts is the ticket to nasty surprises and poor cash flow.

Thoughts About Forecasting, Business, and Money

I love business books. I have amassed a library of over 600 of them (and I add to it every month – Amazon loves me)! I read books with a pen so I can underline and star information that strikes a chord with me. I write notes in them so that I can go back later and scan the parts I need to think more about or reflect on.

Here are some quotes about forecasting, business, and money that I enjoyed from a small sampling of those books. I hope they spark an idea in your mind or just get you thinking more deeply about business. These are also great books to buy and read as well. Enjoy!

My favorite book on financial forecasting is *Future Ready: How to Master Business Forecasting*. It is written by two of the leading experts in performance management, Steve Morlidge and Steve Player. They create a compelling and deep dive into the why and how of forecasting on many different levels (and with many different types of forecasts). It is a fantastic book that you will enjoy reading.

I am the proud owner of an autographed copy of the book from Steve Player!

15 February, 2014

To Philip,

May this book help you and your clients become Future Ready! I look forward to working with you.

Best Regards,

Steve Player

From *Future Ready* by
Steve Morlidge and Steve Player

"This book helps business people improve their ability to forecast the future. By improving your organization's ability to anticipate, you will be better prepared. As a result, you will deliver more reliable performance, and be in better shape to exploit opportunities and avoid potential catastrophes."

"…The purpose of forecasting is to help 'steer the ship'. By providing information about the likely future position, we can decide either to do nothing different, or we can change our plans, and so, 'change the future'. You can only do this by doing something different, and doing something different usually involves some combination of:

- Stopping an existing activity.
- Starting a new (unplanned) activity.
- Speeding up a planned activity.
- Delaying a planned activity.
- Changing a planned activity."

"Decision-making is driven by performance—without it, management is no more than guesswork—and it comes in two ways, there's information about the past (actuals) and then there's information about the future (forecasts)."

"The decision to cross the road involves a forecast—we ask ourselves 'Will that car arrive before I have reached the other side?' This forecast is constantly updated with new information, which we use to adjust our actions; we may speed up, slow down or turn back. In fact, almost every act requires a forecast of some sort; a source of 'information about the future'."

"When making decisions, we cannot rely solely on information about what has happened, we need information about what we believe might happen as well; information that we create through the process of forecasting."

"We might *think* that we want to 'know the future', but in reality we only want to know the future in order to be able to do something about it. In other words, we want to *change* the future to make it more acceptable to us."

"The purpose of forecasting is...to help create the future rather than to predict it."

"There's only one thing we know for sure about a forecast. It is likely to be wrong."

"While it might not be possible to forecast uncertainty, the process of forecasting helps enormously because *in the act of considering possibilities, we enhance our awareness.*"

From *Implementing Beyond Budgeting: Unlocking the Performance Potential (2nd Edition) By Bjarte Bogsnes*

"A target is *what we want* to happen; a forecast is what we *think will happen*, whether we like what we see or not. Forcing a target and a forecast into being one number in one process is almost guaranteed to result in either a bad target or a bad forecast or both..."

"A forecast is *not* a promise, not something to deliver on. People using that expression have not understood the difference between a forecast and a target. Again, a forecast is what we think will happen, an *expectation*; a target is what we want to happen, an *aspiration.*"

"Some would call 'on course to hit a rock' a bad forecast. Assuming it is true, it is a *good* forecast, even though it contains bad news."

"Forecasting should primarily be something *you do for yourself* to help you manage your own business."

"A forecast should also be *actionable.* If the information cannot be used to trigger any action, why do we forecast?"

"I would much rather have good forecasts with bad news than a bad forecast with good news."

"It is quite natural to have *gaps* between ambitious targets and realistic forecasts."

From *Superforecasting* by Philip E. Tetlock and Dan Gardner

"We are all forecasters. When we think about changing jobs, getting married, buying a home, making an investment, launching a product, or retiring, we decide based on how we expect the future will unfold. These expectations are forecasts."

"…We never truly know what will happen next. Hence forecasting is all about estimating the likelihood of something happening."

"How predictable something is depends on what we are trying to predict, how far into the future, and under what circumstances."

"Weather forecasts are typically quite reliable, under most conditions, looking a few days ahead, but they become increasingly less accurate three, four, and five days out."

From *Best Practices in Planning and Performance Management* by David A. J. Axson

"When asked to construct a forecast, the fact that most are wrong is perhaps the hardest concept for most people to come to terms with."

"The real value of a forecast is not the accuracy of the answer, but the insights into how current decisions and future events interact to shape performance."

"Positioning the forecast process as a decision support tool that seeks to provide insight into future opportunities and threats reduces the pressure to develop absolutely precise estimates. As a general rule, the level of detail in a forecast should decrease the farther out you look. In the last few years, best practice organizations...are forecasting more frequently and reducing the amount of detail in each forecast."

"Providing time for management to plan how it will react under different sets of circumstances is one of the biggest benefits of the whole forecast process."

"The forecast is not simply an extrapolation of the financial plan. The financial forecast is derived directly from the forecast of key business drivers."

FROM *BILLION DOLLAR COMPANY* BY ROBERT H. HACKER

". . . Now, if we were to ask what are the two or three most important questions that a business plan or financial model should answer, somewhere in the top three would probably be 'how much money do you need and for what?'"

"I have come to realize that managing the business by focusing on the growth drivers is a sound and understandable management approach and would help entrepreneurs to focus on what is important."

FROM *THE SIX-MONTH FIX* BY GARY SUTTON

"The function of a business is to create money, not consume it, and the longer you postpone this the harder it gets to fix."

"Bankers cannot make more than a few percentage points on the money loaned, but they can lose it all. That's why they're jumpy. They make more money by avoiding losses than by getting new clients. Help them relax by getting them familiar with your business."

"Receivables are viewed as nothing more than test market expenses until they are paid. There is no sale assumed, no customer satisfaction believed, and no commission paid until the money arrives."

"Converting Controllers to CFOs is…tough. The skills are the same but the personality is different, and even the Mayo Clinic isn't performing personality transplants just yet. Controllers set budgets, squeeze dollars, and control. CFOs sell forecasts. One sells the outside world. The other squeezes internally."

FROM *THE WAY TO WEALTH* BY BRIAN TRACY

"All business relationships are built on trust. Since all of business involves money—from bankers, suppliers, vendors, shareholders, and investors—and the opinions of customers and clients, the most important single ingredients for success in business are trust and credibility."

"Your ultimate goal in business is to reach the point where you have enough money so that you never have to worry about money again."

"This means you have to be measuring your success by the amount of money you are able to take out of the business and put somewhere smart and safe, ideally in appreciating or income-generating assets."

From *How to Sell at Margins Higher Than Your Competitors* by Lawrence L. Steinmetz, PhD., and William T. Brooks

"Products and services are sold—and prices stick—because a business gives its customers quality, service, and on-time delivery. And these companies that know how to create a brand and promote and sell those three things—quality, service, and on-time delivery—will have prospects wanting to do business with them. But all those things cost money. If you are going to give your customers what they need and want, you've got to charge a premium price."

"Have you ever worked for an unprofitable business? If you have, you probably learned that it's not much fun. Perhaps people who work at unprofitable businesses should consider putting signs in their offices that say, 'It ain't fun if it ain't profitable.' If you have worked for both profitable and unprofitable businesses, we think you would agree it's more fun when the enterprise is actually making money. We have never heard anybody complain about excessive frugality in successful businesses; but we sure have heard about 'the need to tighten up' in an unprofitable one."

"Just remember, if you want to stay viable and make some money, you'd better be prepared to be a little bit aggressive on price. This means you really do have to raise your price on a regular basis."

From *Your Money & Your Brain* by Jason Zweig

"Making money feels good, all right; it just doesn't feel as good as expecting to make money. In a cruel irony that has enormous implications for financial behavior, your investing brain comes equipped

with a biological mechanism that is more aroused when you anticipate a profit than when you actually get one."

FROM *THE 80/20 PRINCIPLE*
BY RICHARD KOCH

"Accounting systems are the enemy of fair rewards, because they
are absolutely brilliant at obscuring where the money is really being
made. This is why, human frailty apart, the imbalance between performance and reward is greater in large and complex firms than in
small businesses."

"My view is that money is not difficult to obtain, and, once you
have even a little of it to spare, it is not difficult to multiply."

FROM *E-MYTH MASTERY*
BY MICHAEL E. GERBER

"After almost 30 years, passionately pursuing the quixotic subject
of business, I have come to the steadfast conclusion that there is
nothing in the creation and operation of a company that so seem-
ingly conspires to confuse, intimidate, overwhelm, complicate, ratio-
nalize, and metastasize the plain ignorance of the average business
guy, or woman, than money."

"What I've discovered is that most owners and managers ignore
the money until it's too late to ignore it, and then become frantic to
fix what needed to be fixed all along, but wasn't. And as soon as they
fix it, if they're lucky enough to get a second chance, they go right
back to sleep again."

From *Loving What Is* by Byron Katie

"When I argue with reality, I lose—but only 100% of the time."

"Arguing with reality is like trying to teach a cat to bark—hopeless."

"If I think you're my problem, I'm insane."

"I'm a lover of what is, not because I'm a spiritual person, but because it hurts when I argue with reality."

"Thoughts aren't personal. They just appear, like raindrops. Would you argue with a raindrop?"

"When we stop opposing reality, action becomes simple, fluid, kind, and fearless."

"We're often quite sure about what other people need to do, how they should live, whom they should be with. We have 20/20 vision about other people, but not about ourselves."

"Once you see the truth, the thought lets go of you, not the other way around."

"Reality rules, whether we're aware of it or not."

From *Simple Numbers, Straight Talk, Big Profits!* by Greg Crabtree

"One of the skill sets that we've built into our firm is the ability to forecast and quantify every situation. We believe that you have to play out multiple scenarios—actually plan out those cash flows—

206

and create reasonable expectations for the investor. Will it take eighteen months for the investors to get their money back? Or will it take five years?"

"This is probably contrary to what many others think, but I believe that once you get to a million dollars of revenue, you'd better be profitable and paying yourself a market-based wage."

"It is not sufficient to just forecast net income; you also need to forecast cash flows and capital requirements."

"You can't build wealth until you get out of debt. And make no mistake getting out of debt really does help you build wealth."

"Do not confuse debt with capital. Capital is the cash you leave in the business to fund your receivables and inventory for normal business conditions, and debt is financing for special cases."

"Cash is the most powerful opportunity magnet ever created."

"If the business makes a profit beyond your salary, the business should make a tax distribution to cover the taxes it caused you to pay."

THE *DESTINATION WEDDING SPECIALIST*

The next few quotes are not from a book. They are from a talented business owner who has navigated a changing industry and created a thriving, growing business. Lauré Poffenberger owns a niche travel agency that specializes in Destination Weddings and luxury travel. Destination Weddings are a growing trend because couples can marry in a beautiful setting while also providing a fun, relaxing, and memorable experience for their family and friends. Lauré is the Destination Wedding Guru (and my wife)!

Here are just a few of her words of wisdom about business and money (and travel).

"You can't smell urine on the internet."

"People travel one or two notches above how they live."

"You don't want to be on vacation...and wish you were home."

"I know you believe you understand what you think I said but I'm not sure you realize that what I said is not what I meant."

"Life is still life—even in paradise."

"Self-employed can equal unemployed if you are not focused on making money."

You can learn more about Lauré and her Destination Wedding and Romantic, Luxury Included Travel services at: www.travelcruisevacations.com/destination-weddings/.

Your Feedback Is Valuable

When I read a book I really enjoy, I try to find the author's email address and send them a note to tell them how much I appreciate the information and insight in their book. I'm certain that most authors appreciate feedback from readers. But you wouldn't know it based on how hard it is to find contact information for the author in their book!

So I'm making it easy for you because I would absolutely love to hear your feedback about this book. Did you love it? Did you hate it? Are you going to use financial forecasting to drive growth, profitability, and cash flow in your business?

You can send me feedback or questions at pcampbell@financialrhythm.com or pcampbellcfo@gmail.com. You can call or send a text message at 512.944.3520. I would be honored to hear from you.

The figures and graphics in the book were created by Rachel DiMatteo of Majestic Design. Rachel is a very talented graphic designer (and a lot of fun to work with). You can contact Rachel at majesticdesign7@gmail.com.

Free Downloads and Examples

As a CEO I worked for used to say to me, "If it was easy, Philip, anyone could do it." Winning in business isn't easy. It takes a strong business model, a solid strategy, great execution, and a lot of hard work. (Not to mention a few good breaks along the way.)

And forecasting can be hard work . . . at least in the beginning.

To make the work of getting started just a little easier, I invite you to visit the companion website for this book at www.ILoveForecasting.com. The Excel forecasting model used in the forecasting example is there for you to download. There are additional examples, tools, tips, and tricks to help you get your forecasting process up and running.

I have a website at http://financialrhythm.com dedicated to entrepreneurs and business owners and their advisors. It is a place to get simple, actionable strategies for creating a financial future that is bigger and brighter than your past. You can create a free membership account that gets you access to tips, tools, reports, and videos all devoted to helping you drive growth, profitability, and cash flow higher and higher every year.

As I say in my book *Never Run Out of Cash*, "Either you do the work or have someone else do it." That is the formula for getting things done. The free resources I have provided online for you will help you and your CFO, controller, outside CPA, or other consultants that you engage to get started.

But if you get stuck, or you have a hard time lining up the resources or advisors to help you, send me an email at pcampbell@ financialrhythm.com or pcampbellcfo@gmail.com and I will happily point you in the right direction.

Books and Online Courses
by Philip Campbell

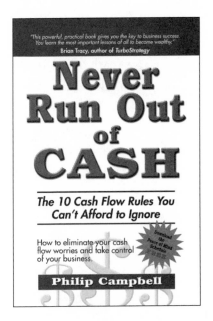

NEVER RUN OUT OF CASH: THE 10 CASH FLOW RULES YOU CAN'T AFFORD TO IGNORE

"This powerful, practical book gives you the key to business success. You learn the most important lessons of all to become wealthy."

—BRIAN TRACY, *TurboStrategy*

213

"This is a revolutionary money-management book. Throw out all the other complicated methods of handling projections and financial strategizing—use Philip's Peace of Mind schedule to get just that— Peace of Mind about your cash flow!"

—DR. JOE VITALE, BEST-SELLING AUTHOR

You will see your business in a whole new light after you learn these principles and put them into action. Here are just a few of the skills and techniques you will learn:

- The four secrets for creating cash flow projections you can trust.
- How you can use the Peace of Mind schedule to create an almost magical feeling of control.
- The simple process for ensuring your cash balance is accurate.
- How to dramatically increase the quality of your business decisions.
- How the Peace of Mind schedule fills the enormous gap that the standard financial statements create.
- How to recognize and understand the cash flow "timing differences" in your business.
- How to use the "Smell Test" and the "90% Test" to create an amazingly accurate estimate of what your cash balance will be six months from now.
- How to avoid falling into the trap of worrying about your money.

I'm super-excited to be sharing it with you.

Grab your copy NOW at your favorite online bookstore.
Or got to www.NeverRunOutOfCash.com. You'll love it.

Understanding Your Cash Flow – In Less Than 10 Minutes

This online course teaches you a simple, step-by-step approach to understanding and managing your cash flow. Here are the two unique promises I make to you in this course:

1. I'll show you how to understand your cash flow in less than 10 minutes.

2. I'll show you how to explain what happened to your cash last month to your business partner or banker (or maybe even your spouse) in a 2-minute conversation.

I take off my CPA hat and speak in the language every business owner can relate to. No jargon. No stuffy financial rambling. Just a simple, common sense approach that only takes 10 minutes a month.
   The course includes:

- **The video presentation of the course.** This is a screencast that you can watch and listen to on your favorite device. I walk you through the step-by-step process and show you how to understand your cash flow in less than 10 minutes a month.
- **The course workbook.** This is a downloadable workbook to help you get a fast start with the course material. It has all the examples and everything you need to complete your first Cash Flow Focus Report.
- **The Cash Flow Focus Report.** You get the links to download the PDF or spreadsheet version of the Cash Flow Focus Report. Just 10 minutes a month with this unique and simple tool and you will wonder how you ever got by without it.
- **The slides from the presentation.** You can download a document with a copy of each slide from the presentation so you can

215

go back to any specific example or portion of the recorded presentation.

I provide a no questions asked, 100% refund guarantee with the course. If you don't love the course, I'll refund 100% of the purchase price.

Learn more about the course at http://financialrhythm.com/cash-flow-course/